Set a pretty table forty with these nap~~kins~~

A table setting that showcases your beautifully folded napkins invites your guests to share in the spirit of your party, whether your theme is elegant or casual, fun or romantic, retro-funky or up-to-the-minute chic. For every occasion and party theme, there's a napkin fold that will make it even more memorable and fun. Here are just a few ways you can incorporate the napkin folds in this book into a fabulous table setting for your event.

Birthday for a Special Mom

Pope's Hat (page 78)

Heart (page 146)

Bouquet (page 30)

Tropics (page 220)

Southern Charm

Herb Pot (page 148)

Fleur (page 142)

Shield (page 90)

Two Points (page 114)

Barcelona Bash

Duet (page 54)

Orchid 2 (page 214)

Fish (page 140)

Stairway (page 174)

Afternoon Tea

Orchid 1 (page 156)

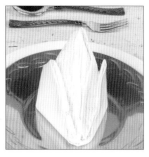
Dutch Baby (page 206)

Two Points (page 114)

Vase (page 118)

Italian Pasta Party

Duet (page 54)

Trifold (page 110)

Divided Square (page 50)

Diamonds (page 46)

Girls' Night In

Clown Hat (page 128)

Bikini (page 24)

Bouquet (page 30)

African Ivory Coast

Divided Fan (page 48)

Ring Roll (page 82)

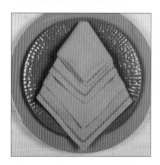
Gypsy Skirt (page 62)

Grecian Get Together

The Standard (page 100)

Ring Roll (page 82)

Pinwheel (page 164)

High Tower (page 150)

German Feast

Luna Moth (page 212)

Bird in Flight (page 26)

Fish (page 140)

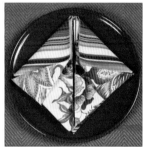
Reveal (page 170)

Champagne and Caviar Party

Peacock (page 162)

Two Tails (page 116)

Clutch (page 40)

Pacific Northwest Coast

Clamshell (page 204)

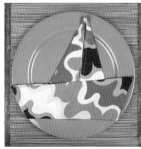
Sailboat (page 88)

Wave (page 188)

Chinese Banquet

Bowtie (page 34)

Divided Fan (page 48)

Fortune Cookie (page 60)

Fan (page 56)

Turkish Twilight

Duet (page 54)

Orchid 2 (page 214)

Stairway (page 174)

Pope's Hat (page 78)

Mexican Fiesta

Burro (page 38)

Parrot (page 160)

Pleat (page 74)

Hawaiian Luau

Aloha Shirt (page 198)

Bird of Paradise (page 202)

Simply Skinny (page 96)

Friends' Game Night

Bouquet (page 30)

Buffet Roll (page 36)

Oscar Night

Clutch (page 40)

Tuxedo (page 182)

Super Bowl Party

Cup Kerchief (page 44)

Buffet Roll (page 36)

Western Hoedown

Hobo Sack (page 64)

Pocket (page 76)

Wine and Cheese Tasting

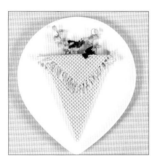

Vase (page 118)

Triple Layer (page 180)

Fleur de Lis (page 144)

Neighborhood Block Party

Ring Roll (page 82)

Pocket (page 76)

Buffet Roll (page 36)

Picnic Boxed Lunch

Tie One On (page 106)

The Standard (page 100)

Kids' Treasure Hunt

Placemat (page 72)

Loot Bag (page 68)

Garden Brunch

Simple Upright (page 92)

Bird's Nest (page 28)

Diagonal (page 132)

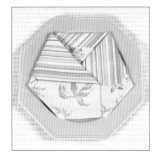

Shawl (page 172)

Liner (page 66)

Top 100 step-by-step
Napkin Folds

Top 100 step-by-step
Napkin Folds

More than 1,000 Photographs

Denise Vivaldo

Robert
ROSE

Top 100 Step-by-Step Napkin Folds
Text copyright © 2012 Denise Vivaldo
Cover and text design copyright © 2012 Robert Rose Inc.

The material in this book was previously published in *Perfect Table Settings* by Denise Vivaldo, published by Robert Rose in 2010.

For complete cataloguing information, see page 224.

Design and Production: Andrew Smith and Joseph Gisini/PageWave Graphics Inc.
Editor: Sue Sumeraj
Proofreader: Sheila Wawanash

All photography except pages listed below:
  Jon Edwards and Associates / © 2012 Denise Vivaldo
Art direction and styling by Denise Vivaldo and Cindie Flannigan

Page 10: ©iStockphoto.com/Kieran White; 13: ©iStockphoto.com/Lisa Thornberg; 14: ©iStockphoto.com/ Lisa Thornberg; 17: ©iStockphoto.com/Jill Chen.

We acknowledge the financial support of the Government of Canada through the Book Publishing Industry Development Program (BPIDP) for our publishing activities.

Published by Robert Rose Inc.
120 Eglinton Avenue East, Suite 800, Toronto, Ontario, Canada M4P 1E2
Tel: (416) 322-6552 Fax: (416) 322-6936
www.robertrose.ca

Printed and bound in China

1 2 3 4 5 6 7 8 9 PPLS 20 19 18 17 16 15 14 13 12

Contents

Acknowledgments

I grew up with a mother who loved to set the table. China, flowers, linens — it didn't have to be a special occasion; at our house, a beautifully set table was an everyday occurrence. Thanks, Mom, for teaching me to enjoy pretty things and sharing your gift of making guests happy and comfortable. This book is as much yours as it is mine.

Writing and completing any book is a team effort. I am grateful that I get to work with so many talented people; otherwise, I wouldn't do it! For me, the two best days of any book deal are the day I sign the contract and the day I hold my first copy of the finished book in my hot, greedy little hands. The days in between are a blur of frustration, elation and exhaustion. I equate writing books to babysitting: I like it best when the baby is clean, quiet and put to bed.

This book could not have happened without my friend Jon Edwards, a talented and generous photographer. Not only did Jon shoot most of the images in this book, but he worked hand in hand with the publisher, sending roughly 2,000 images over the course of six months. He never said, "No, I can't help you today, Denise," even on days when he saw us darkening his studio door with tubs and boxes of napkins and props. Jon's associate at his studio, Heather Winters, a great photographer in her own right, helped us in too many ways to count. I thank you both so very much.

Speaking of us, the nimble and talented hands you see in the how-to napkin fold photos belong to Cindie Flannigan and Jennifer Park, the world's best hand models (and worst-paid) ever! Miss Cindie's nickname is "Busy Hands," and there isn't a napkin she can't wrangle. Many of the napkin folds were Cindie's invention or redesign. Sit her down in front of a stack of napkins and she can't help herself. My napkin fold experience came from my years in catering, where any napkin fold you can teach a waiter in two minutes is a keeper. Our darling assistant, Jennifer Park, tackled many of the more difficult folds. She's still young and limber! You two exceptional women know this book wouldn't have gotten into print without you!

To everyone connected with Robert Rose, I hope you enjoyed this experience as much as we did. Thank you.

To Lisa Ekus, you and your group rock! I'd be hard-pressed to find a better friend and agent. And thank you, Lisa, for tolerating my complaints all those times I forgot how lucky I am. I should have designed the "Gag fold" for myself.

Thanks to Martha Hopkins for her constant support and unbelievable help. She serves excellent advice with humor, even when the ship is going down. I'm only sorry the captain of the *Titanic* didn't have Martha at his side instead of a band.

To Laura Meyn, Kristen Green Wiewora and Mandy Unruh, please don't change your phone numbers. Martha, Cindie and I need you three!

And last but not least, to my husband, Ken Meyer, a man who appreciates a cloth napkin even when I haven't cooked dinner. As he says, a cloth napkin always gives him hope.

— Denise Vivaldo

Introduction

Knowing how to execute a perfect napkin fold is not a skill everyone has, but it's one you can easily and quickly teach yourself — with the help of this book, of course. These days, anything other than the typical rectangular napkin fold is an uncommon touch for at-home entertaining, yet napkin folds can bring a touch of elegance, whimsy or retro style to your table. And napkin folds take your table setting to the next level with no added expense — you'd have napkins on the table anyway; you're just learning dozens of clever new ways to present them.

Cloth napkins can serve a number of purposes on the table beyond the obvious, acting as placemats, vases or favor bags, for example. No matter which fold you choose — and whether it's on the table for a child's birthday party or a sophisticated dinner party for grownups — the result will make your event more memorable. Like a handwritten thank-you note, napkin folds might be less common than they once were, but they're always noticed, always appreciated and always in style.

The 100 step-by-step napkin folds in this book are divided into easy, intermediate and advanced sections, so you'll know which ones to start with and how to work your way up. Remember that simpler is sometimes better. The most formal folds, in fact, tend to be relatively easy. And when you're using napkins with an elaborate pattern or design, a simple fold may show it off the best.

While crisp, clean lines are important in the execution of a successful napkin fold, do remember that it's a napkin, not a permanent installation. When your guest sits down, the napkin will be whipped out of shape and draped across a lap, so it doesn't have to be architecturally sound, just a fun but fleeting artistic touch.

Napkin Folds 101

Why take the time for napkin folds? A table set with carefully folded cloth napkins simply makes your guests feel special. Napkin folds certainly add style to the table, but they also warmly evoke the personal touches of another time — one when attention to every detail prevailed over convenience. As a longtime professional caterer and food stylist, it's my job to pay attention to the little details that make a big difference. But there's no reason why you can't do it at home, too. While the popularity of napkin folding comes and goes, I refuse to see it as a lost art. Spend an hour or two with this book, and you can easily teach yourself a number of folds that will help you create a table that is timelessly elegant, retro-funky or up-to-the-minute chic. And if you think napkin folds are only for cruise ships, consider this: adding artfully folded cloth napkins to your tabletop will delight your guests, cost you nothing extra and eliminate disposable paper napkins from your repertoire, greening your entertaining style. How's that for modern?

Choosing the Right Napkins

To get started, all you need is a set of cloth napkins, which you might already have. Otherwise, begin with an easy-on-the-budget set. Medium-weight cotton napkins in a light, neutral color are versatile and chic. If that seems too plain, remember that a fresh flower, place card or wrapped candy tucked into the fold can add color or style to the table when your linens are subtler, as can a napkin ring, colorful ribbon or tassel.

Fabrics

Cloth napkins add sumptuous texture to the table and are more elegant and more absorbent than their paper counterparts. Since you can reuse them for years or even decades, they're environmentally friendly, too. But not all cloth is created equal: napkins come in a number of different fabrics, from 100% linen, cotton or polyester to a variety of blends that attempt to capture the most desirable aspects of each material. Before buying cloth napkins, consider how a particular fabric feels on your hands and face, how well it will go with your china and what kind of care it requires.

Fabric also comes in a variety of weights, from very light to very heavy, and certain weights perform better for certain napkin folds. While a very simple fold can look fuller when done with a thick napkin, a more complicated fold might work better with a thinner napkin that won't get too bulky with multiple folded layers. Each of the 100 napkin folds in this book indicates the weight of fabric it will work best with, so if you have a particular fold in mind, shop for the napkin that will show it off best.

Linen

While a set of white linen napkins, preferably monogrammed, used to be de rigueur for elegant entertaining, linen napkins are usually the most expensive and always require thorough ironing. Linen is made from the flax plant, which has stronger fibers than cotton. Linen is a refined, elegant and cool material, and it's durable; over time and with repeated washings, it will get softer. While linen is infamous for its propensity to wrinkle, it irons to a crisp, cool texture that cotton or polyester can only dream of. If you're lucky enough to have a set of linen napkins, whether new or inherited, use them to add elegance to a special gathering.

Cotton

Absorbent, economical and soft, 100% cotton is probably the most popular choice for cloth napkins for at-home entertaining. While they usually need to be ironed for company, if they're removed from the dryer and folded promptly, many cotton napkins will be presentable for daily family use without ironing. Cotton napkins are also widely available — you'll find them at discount stores as well as high-end retailers, in a variety of colors and patterns, from very elegant to very casual, and in a variety of weights, from light to heavy. Keep in mind that cotton cloth in darker colors will fade with repeated washings, so start with a light neutral.

Polyester

Less absorbent and less sumptuous than their natural-fiber counterparts, polyester napkins can evoke an institutional food-service feel, rougher to the touch than cotton or linen. That said, they can usually be used without ironing, they're resistant to fading and staining, and they're inexpensive. Some polyester fabrics are too soft to hold a crease, though, and are therefore not a good choice for many napkin folds, especially those that are designed to stand upright.

Everyday Cloth Napkins

Some families use cloth napkins every day, taking their commitment to going green so seriously that they even pack cloth napkins in their kids' lunch boxes. For such uses, any cotton napkin will do — lunch boxes are a great venue for mismatched napkins from your own collection or those on sale at home goods stores. It's a good idea to use napkins that aren't special, as one might go missing on occasion.

Blends

As you shop for napkins, you'll find linen-cotton blends and cotton-polyester blends, all of which aim to capitalize on the attributes of each component fabric, whether for color-fastness, texture, thrift or easy care. To keep blends looking their best, always read the care instructions for washing and ironing.

Other Fabrics

Napkins can be made of nearly any fabric. Hemp is gaining momentum; like linen, it's a strong natural fiber, and it's machine-washable. You'll also find silk napkins, which are suitable for some napkin folds, bringing a special sheen to the table.

Colors, Styles and Embellishments

While a crisp white linen or cotton napkin is a great basic supply and works best for the most formal folds, patterns and colors feel less stuffy for many occasions, bringing visual interest to the table and making for stylish folds that fit modern sensibilities. Most of us seek out matching sets of napkins, but a variety of similar patterns can be even more interesting, as can two or more alternating solid colors for larger gatherings. Some hosts even lay out two different folds at each place, making the table setting more dynamic.

When shopping for napkins, in addition to looking at fabric, color and pattern, you'll want to look at the construction of the napkins to determine their quality and suitability for your table. Following are some additional aspects of napkin design to look for.

Make Your Own Embellished Napkins

Bored with a set of neutral cloth napkins? A sewing machine makes quick work of adding trim to napkins, and grosgrain ribbon, colorful rickrack or sassy pom-pom trim will completely change their look. Be sure to prewash both trim and napkins before beginning, as materials can shrink at different rates. While more time-consuming, embroidery is also a great way to embellish cloth napkins.

To add character to napkins without breaking out needle and thread, try fabric markers, which work well on cotton or polyester. These permanent markers can be used freehand or with stencils to add a motif to the edges of napkins or all over them, instantly perking them up. Not much of an artist? Use words to add interest: quotable phrases, poetry, astrological signs and fortune cookie–style admonitions can be written around the edges in any color you choose. Experiment on paper first to make sure you get the spacing as you want it.

Hemmed Edges

Most cotton and linen napkins have hemmed edges, where the edges are folded over and seamed for an elegant finish. Some polyester napkins simply have serged edges, where the edges of the material are bound in thread to keep them from fraying. Hemmed edges look more upscale than serged edges.

Embellished Edges

Some of the most charming vintage linens are embellished with hand-crocheted or lacy edges. Even handkerchiefs with hand-crocheted trim can be folded into quarters to use as cocktail napkins. You'll find many modern versions of napkins with embellished edges too, including those with fringe or beaded trim. Some napkin folds (such as Simplicity, page 94) show off embellished edges better than others, so choose folds that make the most of your napkins.

Hemstitched Napkins

Usually made of linen or hemp, hemstitched napkins are characterized by a wide hem that is attached to the main portion of the napkin with a series of delicate geometric stitches. Hemstitched linens are typically sold in solid colors, and they have a classic, elegant look. They are widely available at retailers such as Pottery Barn (www.potterybarn.com) and Williams-Sonoma (www.williams-sonoma.com).

Damask Napkins

While they can be made of linen, cotton, silk, rayon or even polyester, damask napkins are defined by their woven patterns. Look for a satin weave atop a flat background, usually in the same color, where only the sheen of the fabric reveals the tone-on-tone design. Damask napkins have a very formal look. Their patterns are often intricate floral motifs.

Monogrammed Napkins

Monogrammed napkins bring old-world elegance to the table. While a set of white linen napkins with a white monogram used to be a customary, if very generous, wedding gift, such a set is less commonly found in today's households (outside the Deep South in the United States). If you have your grandmother's set, or you happen upon a vintage set, use them whether or not they bear your own initials — vintage linens are usually very soft and always bring added charm to the table, and an unfamiliar monogram can kick off a fun conversation (who *was* DSS?). Some napkin folds show off a monogram better than others; try Two Points (page 114) for a corner monogram.

Size

Perfectly symmetrical square napkins work best for creating napkin folds. Shoppers will likely notice that, while most cloth napkins are square, not all cloth napkins are the same size; in fact, there doesn't seem to be a universal standard. In general, the larger the meal, the larger the napkin should be. For most of the napkin folds in this book, you'll want a napkin that is at least 20 inches (50 cm) square.

Cocktail Napkins

Used flat as a sort of coaster or folded as a napkin, cocktail napkins can range anywhere from 6 to 13 inches (15 to 33 cm) square. The smaller ones aren't much use for folding, though they make an elegant alternative to paper cocktail napkins when set under a drink.

Luncheon Napkins

Larger than cocktail napkins but smaller than dinner napkins, luncheon napkins range from 12 to 20 inches (30 to 50 cm) square, where they get into dinner napkin territory. Luncheon napkins will work well with some folds, but those on the smaller end aren't usually ample enough for complicated folds.

Dinner Napkins

The largest napkins are the most versatile for napkin folding and can certainly be used at a brunch or lunch as easily as they can at dinner. Dinner napkins are typically 20 to 24 inches (50 to 60 cm) square, although vintage linens and custom-made napkins can be even larger.

Paper Napkins

For the most part, cloth napkins are preferable to paper; they're more absorbent, more eco-friendly and more elegant. But there are times when the convenience of paper napkins will make them your first choice. Paper napkins come in an endless supply of solid colors and colorful patterns, as well as in personalized printed versions that are a nice way to commemorate special occasions such as weddings, anniversaries or reunions.

- **Paper cocktail or beverage napkins** are usually around 5 inches (13 cm) square — about 10 inches (25 cm) when unfolded. These are small enough that they're best left in their folded state and used under drinks.
- **Paper luncheon napkins**, which are typically 6 to $6\frac{1}{2}$ inches (15 to 16 cm) square — or up to 13 inches (33 cm) when unfolded — are the right size and shape for use in place of cloth napkins for certain napkin folds. Some companies offer more

generous dinner-size versions of these napkins, up to 8 inches (20 cm) square when folded. Remember that once you have folded a paper napkin, the crease is there to stay, so practice your fold a few times on the same napkin before getting started on the ones you intend to place on the table. Designs that begin by folding the napkin into a smaller square, such as the Shield (page 90) or even the Bird of Paradise (page 202), are good candidates for paper napkins, because their permanent creases won't detract from the finished design.

- **Paper dinner napkins** are often rectangular, roughly $8\frac{1}{2}$ by $4\frac{1}{2}$ inches (21 by 11 cm) folded. Rectangular napkins won't work for most of the napkin folds in this book. Some paper dinner napkins are square when unfolded; read the package carefully to see whether they're square or rectangular when open. Either way, folded paper dinner napkins can be rolled around flatware and tied with ribbon for a quick version of a buffet roll.

- **Paper guest towels** are similar in size to rectangular paper dinner napkins, but they're a thicker weight, suitable for drying hands. In fact, paper can be preferable to cloth in the guest bath: at larger gatherings where a single cloth towel would be used many times, paper is a more sanitary choice. Paper guest towels can look quite elegant stacked in a basket in your guest bathroom; look for those preprinted with a single initial, as a nod to monogrammed linens.

Napkin Rings

Want to save trees by using cloth napkins every day? Want to save water (and time) by not washing them every day? Give yourself a push in the right direction by investing in some napkin rings. The original intent of monogrammed silver napkin rings was to identify the napkin of each household member so his or her napkin could be reused, avoiding the labor-intensive task of daily laundering. If that bit of history seems fitting for your busy modern life, consider a set of personalized napkin rings for your own family.

Where to Place Napkins on the Table

Back when formal entertaining reigned, the only places you would find a perfectly folded cloth napkin on a set table would be to the left of the forks or atop the plate at each place setting. These days, it seems, anything goes. Depending upon the napkin fold you choose, it might be perched inside the wine or water glasses, hanging over the backs of chairs, nestled inside bowls or wrapped around the silverware. As long as each guest can easily reach his or her napkin and easily use it for its original purpose (no double-knotted ribbons, please), then it works.

While monogrammed silver napkin rings are the classic, there's no need to get that fancy if it doesn't suit your lifestyle. Craft stores such as Hobby Lobby (www.hobbylobby.com) and some Michaels locations (www.michaels.com) carry unfinished wooden napkin rings that can be painted and then personalized. Finished wooden napkin rings are also available at many home goods stores and are easy to personalize: stencil on monogram-style initials or use a paint pen to decorate them in any freehand style you like. If you're not particularly crafty, just look for mismatched napkin rings that will be easy to tell apart, and let each family member choose one, keeping a few extras on hand for overnight houseguests.

For dinner parties, it's helpful to have a larger set of matched napkin rings to give certain napkin folds, such as the Parasol (page 70), a uniform look. You can use classic metal rings or decorative rings, or you can fashion your own napkin rings with raffia, yarn or ribbon tied around the finished napkin fold. Good places to find inexpensive napkin rings are Cost Plus World Market (www.worldmarket.com), Pier 1 Imports (www.pier1.com), T.J. Maxx (www.tjmaxx.com), Marshalls (www.marshallsonline.com), Ross (www.rossstores.com), Target (target.com), Kohl's (www.kohls.com), Tuesday Morning (www.tuesdaymorning.com), Home Outfitters (www.homeoutfitters.com) and HomeSense (www.homesense.ca).

Easy Napkin Folds

#**1** Airplane

Choose a fun multicolored cloth napkin, like the vivid rainbow-hued design I used here, for a whimsical setup, such as for a child's airplane-themed birthday party or a backyard barbecue. This fold can also bring cool angles to the table for a more grownup sit-down dinner; in that case, select a chic solid-colored cloth napkin. The Airplane fold looks best with pressed napkins; for crisper results, use spray starch.

1 Lay the napkin out as a square, with the finished side facing down and the seamed edges facing up.

2 Fold the lower edge to the upper edge, forming a horizontal rectangle.

3 Holding the center of the lower edge in place with your left hand, use your right hand to fold the right half of the lower edge over to the vertical centerline of the rectangle.

4 Repeat on the left side, folding the lower left edge over to the vertical centerline, forming a triangle.

6 Repeat on the left side, folding the center edge from the vertical centerline down to align with the lower left edge, forming another small triangle.

5 Working with the right side of the triangle, and starting at the vertical centerline, fold the center edge back down to align with the lower right edge, forming a small triangle.

7 Grasping the bottom tip of the large triangle with one hand, use the other hand to gently lift the center of the upper edge so that the smaller triangles at the left and right come in to meet at the vertical centerline.

8 Flatten the lifted fabric into a narrow center triangle that overlaps the small triangles at either side, forming a paper airplane shape.

#❷ BBQ Bib

Some meals are beyond messy. Use an actual barbecue bib or a checkered kitchen towel instead of a napkin for this fold, which suits Southern-style barbecue or seafood boils especially well. The finished fold will look best with medium- to heavyweight fabric, such as the red and white checked bib I used here. Iron bibs or towels lightly without spray starch before folding.

❶ Lay out barbecue bib or kitchen towel vertically, with any ties at the bottom.

❷ Fold the left edge over toward the right edge, slightly less than one-third the width of the bib or towel.

❸ Fold the right edge over toward the left edge, slightly less than one-third the width of the bib or towel, overlapping the previous fold.

❹ Fold the upper edge down to the lower edge, leaving any ties exposed at the bottom.

5 Fold the upper edge down to the lower edge again, leaving any ties exposed at the bottom.

6 Arrange the napkin with any ties (or the open end) at the top.

#❸Bikini

This flirty napkin fold looks just like a bikini bottom, so it's the perfect choice for a summer cocktail party or poolside cookout. Choose a fun, vibrant fabric in any weight, like this napkin with multicolored citrus slices. Iron napkins with spray starch before folding; there's no need to press after folding.

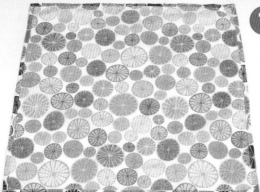

❶ Lay the napkin out as a square, with the finished side facing down and the seamed edges facing up.

❷ Fold the right edge over to the left edge, forming a vertical rectangle.

❸ Fold the lower right and lower left corners in to meet in the center, forming a point at the bottom of the napkin.

❹ Flip the napkin over, keeping the point down.

5 Fold the upper right and upper left corners in to meet in the center, forming a point at the top of the napkin.

6 Fold the upper half of the napkin down over the lower half, leaving about 1 inch (2.5 cm) of the lower half exposed.

7 Fold the upper edge of the napkin down about 2 inches (5 cm), covering where the bottom triangle begins and creating a band on top.

#④ Bird in Flight

This fold is so named because it looks as if it's about to take off into flight. You can use just about any napkin: any weight, fabric, pattern and color will work. Here, I chose a white napkin with maroon and brown flowers. Iron napkins with spray starch before folding. After folding, gently press the tail for a tailored look or leave it as is for a more casual look.

1 Lay the napkin out as a square, with the finished side facing down and the seamed edges facing up.

2 Fold the upper right corner down to the lower left corner, forming a triangle.

3 Fold the lower right point up to the upper left point, forming a smaller triangle.

4 Fold the lowest point up to the highest point, forming an even smaller triangle and arranging the triangle with the loose folds at the top.

5 Fold the upper right point toward the left, using slightly more than two-thirds the width of the napkin and aligning the upper edges.

6 Fold the upper left point back over to the right, aligning the folds at the left edge and allowing the tip to hang past the right edge.

7 Tuck the top 2 inches (5 cm) underneath the napkin, leaving the tail pointing out from the upper right side.

8 Arrange the napkin with the tail at the bottom.

#⑤ Bird's Nest

This little nest will delight guests, and it makes the perfect base for presenting small party favors at each place. Another option is to top each nest with a small bird, whether an edible marshmallow chick in the springtime or a decorative bird ornament come winter. Any fabric weight in any color or pattern will work. Here, I used a yellow napkin with a multicolored leaf pattern. Iron napkins without spray starch before folding.

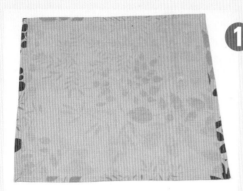

① Lay the napkin out as a square, with the finished side facing down and the seamed edges facing up.

② Fold the lower right corner up to the upper left corner, forming a triangle.

③ Fold the upper left corner down to the middle of the triangle's right side.

④ Fold the upper left edge halfway down to the lower right edge.

⑤ Fold the upper left edge down to the lower right edge, forming a long, narrow napkin.

6 Pick up napkin, with loose edges facing up. Twist the napkin three complete times.

7 Using about half the total length of the twisted napkin, form it into a circle, overlapping the ends.

8 Wrap the loose ends of the napkin around the circle, tucking the tips into the folds of the twisted napkin, forming a nest.

9 Arrange a nest flat at each place.

#⓺ Bouquet

This fold is tied with a ribbon, adding girlish style to the tabletop. Alternatively, you can pull it through a napkin ring. If using ribbon, keep in mind that you will need a 20-inch (50 cm) length for each napkin. Any fabric weight in any color or pattern works; I used a crisp white napkin with a bright multicolored daisy pattern on it and tied it with green- and white-checked ribbon, which would be perfect for a springtime brunch. Press napkins before folding.

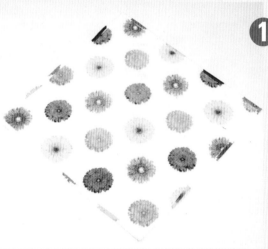

❶ Lay the napkin out as a diamond, with the finished side facing down and the seamed edges facing up.

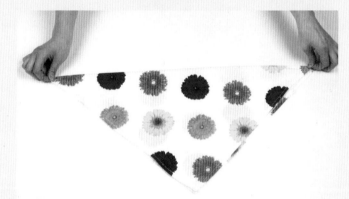

❷ Fold the lower point up to meet the upper point, forming a triangle.

❸ Fold the left point up to the upper point.

❹ Fold the right point up to the upper point, forming a diamond.

5 Wrap a ribbon around the napkin, placing it about one-quarter of the way up from the bottom of the napkin and tying it firmly in a single knot.

6 Tie the ribbon into a bow. Fan out the top layers of fabric.

7 Arrange the napkin with the ribbon at the top or the bottom.

#7Bow

This pretty bow is a great fold for ladies' brunches or lunches, baby showers, bridal showers or anytime you want to bring fun feminine style to the table. I used a solid-colored napkin in a muted yellow hue and paired it with a metal napkin ring. Look for fabrics that contrast with your china, in any color or pattern, and a coordinated napkin ring or tie to hold the bow in place. Stick with light- to medium-weight fabrics so the fold won't be too thick to fit in a napkin ring. Press napkins lightly before folding, but skip the starch in favor of a more flowing look.

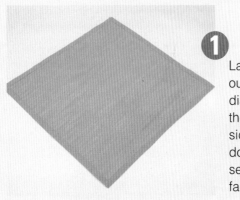

1 Lay the napkin out as a diamond, with the finished side facing down and the seamed edges facing up.

2 Fold lower point of patterned diamond up to upper point of patterned diamond, forming a patterned triangle atop a solid diamond.

3 Fold the lower point up to the upper point, forming a triangle.

4 Fold the lower edge of the napkin up enough to just cover the lower tip of the small triangle.

5 Fold the upper edge of the napkin down to the lower edge.

7 Holding the center of the lower edge with your left hand, use your right hand to fold the right point of the napkin over at an upward angle, making the fold about 2 inches (5 cm) shy of the napkin's vertical centerline and pointing the tail toward the upper left.

6 Repeat on the other side, using your left hand to fold the left point of the napkin over at an upward angle, making the fold about 2 inches (5 cm) shy of the napkin's vertical centerline and pointing the tail toward the upper right.

8 Pinch the center of the fold together with one hand while holding a napkin ring in the other.

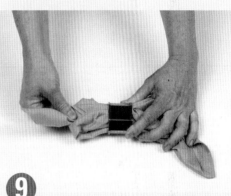

9 Slide the napkin ring over the fold, positioning it in the center.

10 Arrange the bow and tails as necessary. Flip the bow over and arrange it on a plate.

#**8** Bowtie

Simple but very polished-looking, this fold is great for use with napkin rings or ribbons. It works with any color or pattern in almost any fabric weight. I chose brown napkins with purple stripes. Avoid using napkins that are too thick, as the multiple folds will make them difficult to fit through a napkin ring. Iron napkins with spray starch before folding. If the meal requires a pair of chopsticks, slide them between the finished fold and the napkin ring.

1 Lay the napkin out as a square, with the finished side facing down and the seamed edges facing up.

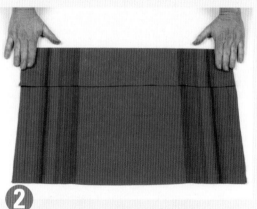

2 Fold the lower edge up to the horizontal centerline of the napkin.

3 Fold the upper edge down to the horizontal centerline.

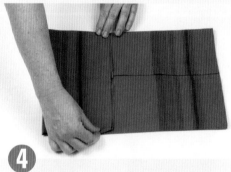

4 Fold the right edge just past the vertical centerline of the napkin.

5 Fold the left edge just past the vertical centerline.

6 Fold the lower edge up about 2 inches (5 cm).

7 Fold the upper edge down about 2 inches (5 cm).

8 Flip the napkin over, keeping the rectangle horizontal. Pinch the middle of the upper edge and lower edge together to form a bow.

9 Slide napkin ring to middle of bow to secure it.

10 If using chopsticks, slide them between the napkin ring and the bow. Present a bow vertically at each place, adjusting the ends as necessary.

#⑨ Buffet Roll

This roll is a neat way to bundle utensils and napkins together, making it easy for your guests to pick up everything they'll need at the end of a buffet line. This fold works with any fabric weight in any color or pattern, but keep in mind that both sides of the fabric will show in the finished roll, so choose something that's attractive on both sides, such as the beige napkin I used here. Iron napkins with spray starch before folding, and tie the finished fold with ribbon to keep utensils securely in place. You'll need a 20-inch (50 cm) length of ribbon for each napkin.

① Lay the napkin out as a square, with the finished side facing down and the seamed edges facing up.

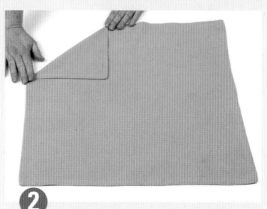

② Fold the lower right corner up about halfway to the center of the napkin.

③ Fold the upper edge of the napkin down to the lower edge, forming a horizontal rectangle.

④ Fold the left edge over to the right edge, forming a square.

⑤ Fold the upper left and right corners in toward the center.

6 Fold the lower left corner in toward the center.

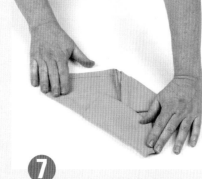

7 Fold the upper right edge down toward the lower left edge just far enough to cover the point.

8 Fold the lower left edge up to the upper right edge.

9 Flip the napkin over, arranging the point at the top.

10 Slide flatware into the pocket and tie the napkin with a ribbon to secure it.

#⑩Burro

You'll need two napkins in slightly different sizes for this attention-grabbing fold — and two napkins per person can be very handy for messy meals. (Fajitas, anyone?) Use light- to medium-weight fabrics in contrasting, festive colors. I paired an orange napkin with a larger, fringed green napkin and placed the finished fold in a beer glass, leaving the ends of the napkin to stick up, looking like two tall burro ears. You can also tie the bottom of the fold with twine or ribbon and lay it flat on each plate. This fold works best with unstarched napkins.

① Lay the smaller napkin out as a square, with the finished side facing down and the seamed edges facing up. Top with the larger napkin, centering it over the first, with the finished side facing down and the seamed edges facing up.

② Rotate the napkins so that they're laid out as a diamond. Fold the lowest corner up to the center of the napkin.

③ Working from the flat fold at the lower end of the diamond, roll napkins up together until you reach the end.

4 Have a beer glass ready as you pick up the napkin from the middle.

5 Fold the napkin in half and drop the folded end into the glass.

6 Arrange the napkin fold so that the ears point up evenly.

#11 Clutch

In the shape of a chic clutch purse, this napkin fold works well with medium- to heavyweight fabric in a feminine pattern, such as the napkin with green and ivory flowers and vines I used here. Decorate the finished fold with a pearl, button or other decorative object to mimic a purse closure. For a completely different look, use a napkin in a bold solid color and call the fold an envelope; use a sticker or foil seal for the closure. Either way, iron the napkins with spray starch before folding; after folding, leave as is for a casual look or press gently for crisp lines.

1 Lay the napkin out as a square, with the finished side facing down and the seamed edges facing up.

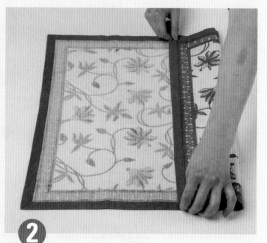

2 Fold the left edge in to the vertical centerline of the napkin.

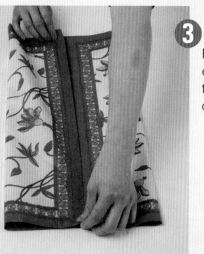

3 Fold the right edge in to the vertical centerline.

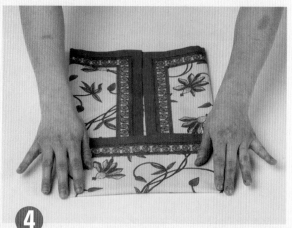

4 Fold the upper edge down to the horizontal centerline of the napkin.

5 Fold the lower edge up to the horizontal centerline.

6 Fold the lower left and right corners in to meet in at the center of the bottom half, forming a point.

7 Fold the point up over the top half of the napkin, forming a clutch shape.

8 Arrange the napkin with the point down. Place a pearl, button or other decorative object where the clutch closure would be.

#12 Crown

This regal fold is fit for celebrating the king or queen of the day, so choose a color worthy of royals, such as the solid red used here — or perhaps lavender or pink for a princess. This fold works best with medium- to heavyweight fabrics ironed with spray starch before folding, because the fabric needs body to stand up (though the crowns can also be displayed flat). Just for fun, place a small treat under the napkin fold to surprise guests.

1 Lay the napkin out as a square, with the finished side facing down and the seamed edges facing up.

2 Fold the lower edge up to the upper edge, forming a horizontal rectangle.

3 Fold the right edge down to the lower edge.

4 Fold the left edge up to the upper edge.

5 Flip the napkin over and arrange it horizontally.

6 Fold the lower edge up to the upper edge, leaving a small triangle dangling on lower left side.

7 Flip the napkin over, arranging it with the triangle still pointing down, but now on the right side. Fold down the small triangle on the left. Fold the left point of the napkin over toward the right, using about one-third the width of the napkin fold and tucking the point under the top layer of fabric.

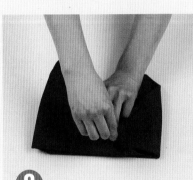

8 Flip the napkin over again, keeping the points down. Fold the left point of the napkin over toward the right, tucking the point under the top layer of fabric.

9 Place flat or stand the crown up, pulling the sides gently apart to create a circular form.

#⓭ Cup Kerchief

Perfect with hot soups or stews, as well as oversize lattes, this cup kerchief acts as a cozy for the bowl or mug, giving it more style as well as protecting hands from the heat. I chose a blue and white fruit print here, but any fabric weight in any color or pattern works with this fold, so choose something that suits the occasion. Iron napkins with spray starch before folding.

1 Lay the napkin out as a square, with the finished side facing down and the seamed edges facing up.

2 Fold the upper left corner down to the lower right corner, forming a triangle.

3 Fold the upper left edge down toward the lower right corner, creating a roughly 2-inch (5 cm) wide band.

4 Wrap the band around a bowl or coffee mug, lacing it through the handle, if there is one.

5 Tie the two tails into a firm single knot around the bowl or mug.

6 Arrange the triangular kerchief as desired.

#**14** Diamonds

A two-sided woven fabric, such as this black napkin with light stripes, works best for the Diamonds fold, because both sides of the napkin will be visible in the finished presentation. Any fabric weight works well. Iron with spray starch before folding; after folding, gently press for a tailored look or leave as is for a more casual look.

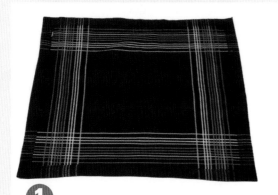

1 Lay the napkin out as a square, with the finished side facing down and the seamed edges facing up.

2 Fold the lower edge up to the upper edge, forming a horizontal rectangle.

3 Fold the right edge over to the left edge, forming a square.

4 Fold the top layer of the upper left corner down to the lower right corner, forming a diagonally divided square.

5 Fold the next layer of the upper left corner down to the center of the napkin, forming a small triangle in the upper left quadrant of the napkin.

6 Fold the top layer of the lower right corner up to the center of the napkin, forming a small triangle in the lower right quadrant of the napkin.

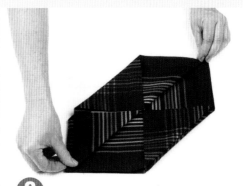

7 Tuck the remaining bottom layers of the lower right corner under the napkin, aligning the edges with the folded top layer.

8 Tuck the remaining bottom layers of the upper left corner under the napkin, aligning the edges with the folded top layer. Arrange the napkin horizontally on a plate.

#⑮Divided Fan

The showy look of this fold is completed with a tie or napkin ring, which gives you another opportunity to incorporate the party's theme. I tied mine off with a piece of raffia and a sand dollar, but you can use any decorative ribbon or yarn, perhaps with a favor or bauble attached. Use a medium- to heavyweight fabric in any color or pattern. I chose a brown napkin with a black pattern. Iron napkins with spray starch before folding, and be sure to have your ties or napkin rings ready before you begin. Use 12-inch (30 cm) lengths if you'll be tying a knot or 20-inch (50 cm) lengths if you'll be tying a bow.

1 Lay the napkin out as a square, with the finished side facing down and the seamed edges facing up.

2 Fold the lower edge up to the horizontal centerline of the napkin.

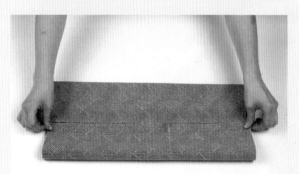

3 Fold the upper edge down to the horizontal centerline.

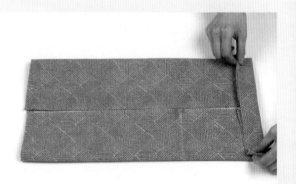

4 Fold the left edge over toward the right, forming a vertical band about 1½ inches (4 cm) wide.

5 Fold the band under, aligning the left edges.

6 Fold the band back over, aligning the left edges.

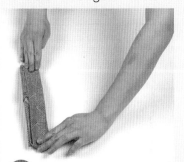

7 Continue folding the band, accordion-style, until you reach the right edge of the napkin.

8 Turn the napkin so that the pleats are facing up and use a tie, ribbon or napkin ring to secure the center.

9 Fan out the folds to create a double fan.

#16 Divided Square

This easy napkin fold is suitable for any occasion and any fabric weight. I chose a traditional ivory and dark red toile napkin here, but you can try this fold with solid, patterned or striped napkins. Iron napkins with spray starch before folding. After folding, gently press for a tailored look or leave as is for a more casual look. To personalize each place, tuck a place card into the opening on this fold. For a different presentation, rotate the square so it's a diamond instead.

1 Lay the napkin out as a square, with the finished side facing down and the seamed edges facing up.

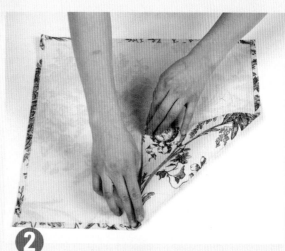

2 Fold the upper left corner to the center of the napkin.

3 Fold the upper right corner to the center.

4 Repeat with the lower left and lower right corners, forming a diamond.

5 Rotate the napkin so that it's laid out as a square. Grip the napkin at the center of both the left and right sides.

6 Carefully lifting the napkin from the sides, tuck the upper half under the lower half, forming a rectangle.

7 Fold the left half over the right half, forming a divided square.

#17 Double Ring

This rolled design brings its understated curves to any place setting. Depending upon the napkin, it could be very formal or informal — you can even set a patio table with this napkin fold. Choose a light- to medium-weight fabric in any design. Napkins with a decorative border are shown off to their best advantage in this fold.

1 Lay the napkin out as a square, with the finished side facing down and the seamed edges facing up.

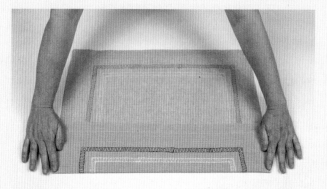

2 Fold the upper edge down to the horizontal centerline of the napkin.

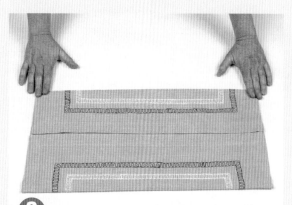

3 Fold the lower edge up to the horizontal centerline, forming a horizontal rectangle.

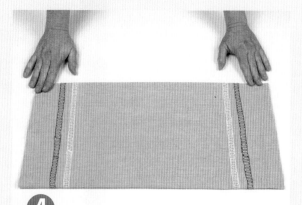

4 Flip the napkin over, keeping it arranged as a horizontal rectangle.

5 Starting at the right edge, roll up the napkin toward the center.

6 Continue rolling until you reach the vertical centerline of the napkin.

7 Beginning at the left edge, roll up the napkin toward the center.

8 Continue rolling until the left roll meets the right roll in the center.

#⓲Duet

This two-napkin fold is easier than it looks. Use silky napkins for a formal look or cotton napkins for a casual table. Medium- to heavyweight fabrics ironed with spray starch work best. Place the napkin fold in a stemmed glass for visual appeal.

1 Use two complementary napkins.

2 Lay the napkins out as a square, with the finished sides facing down and the seamed edges facing up.

3 Line up the napkins so that the edges are aligned.

4 Gather both napkins at the center by placing one hand underneath and pressing the napkins down into your palm with the other hand.

5 Gather about 4 inches (10 cm) together into a loose point.

6 Place the gathered point inside a wineglass or other glass. Pull apart the ends and arrange them as desired.

#⑲Fan

Use a small bowl or mug, or even a takeout box (as on the bottom of page 57), to anchor this easy fold. I chose a solid black napkin and a turquoise blue bowl, but you can use any fabric weight in any color or pattern for this design. Iron napkins with spray starch before folding. Have one container per napkin ready before you begin folding.

❶ Lay the napkin out as a square, with the finished side facing down and the seamed edges facing up.

❷ Fold the lower edge up to the upper edge, forming a horizontal rectangle.

❸ Fold the left and right edges over about 1½ inches (4 cm).

❹ Fold the left and right edges under about 1½ inches (4 cm), aligning the folds at each side.

❺ Fold the left and right edges back over about 1½ inches (4 cm), aligning the folds at each side.

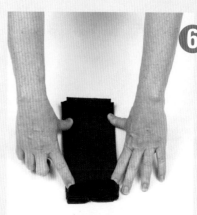

❻ Fold the left and right edges back under about 1½ inches (4 cm) so that they meet under the center of the napkin.

7 Fold the left and right sides together to finish the accordion-style fold.

8 Place the narrow end of the napkin (the one that shows more layers of fabric) in a container, bending it around the bottom of the container to anchor it.

9 Spread out the top of the napkin fold to create a fan effect. Arrange a fan at each place.

#⓴ Fir Tree

Create this easy, fun fold for Christmas, Earth Day or any other party theme that might call for a tree-shaped napkin. To help it stand upright, look for medium- to heavyweight fabrics, and starch and press them before folding. For tree-like results, I chose a solid green napkin, but any solid or pattern will work. For a holiday table, add a Christmas ornament as a favor on each tree — or place a star on top.

1 Lay the napkin out as a square, with the finished side facing down and the seamed edges facing up.

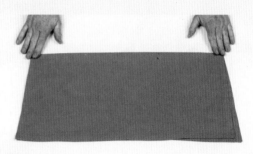

2 Fold the lower edge up to the upper edge, forming a horizontal rectangle.

3 Fold the upper left and lower left corners in to the horizontal centerline, forming a point on the left side.

4 Fold the upper right and lower right corners in to the horizontal centerline, forming a point on the right side.

5 Fold the left point in to the center of the napkin.

6 Fold the right point in to the center, forming a square.

7 Gripping all layers in the center, gently pick up the napkin.

8 Tuck the upper and lower edges in toward the center, forming an upright napkin fold with four points.

9 Arrange the four points.

#21 Fortune Cookie

The Fortune Cookie fold can be placed flat on a plate or displayed upright, with a handwritten fortune tucked inside for each guest. While it would be great for a home-cooked Asian meal, this fold can also elevate takeout. The design works well with fabrics of any weight, color and pattern; I chose a solid aqua napkin. Iron napkins with spray starch before folding; after folding, gently press for a tailored look or leave as is for a more casual look.

1 Lay the napkin out as a diamond, with the finished side facing down and the seamed edges facing up.

2 Fold the upper point down to the lower point, forming a triangle.

3 Holding the middle of the upper edge with your right hand, use your left hand to fold the left point down to the lower point.

4 Fold the right point down to the lower point, forming a diamond.

5 Carefully picking up the napkin from the right and left corners, fold the lower half of the diamond under the upper half, forming a triangle.

6 Gently bring the lower right and left points closer together, raising the napkin to an upright position.

7 Position the napkin on an angle at each place, adding a fortune, if desired.

#22 Gypsy Skirt

This fold looks like a festive multilayered skirt. Use napkins with decorative borders or trim to take full advantage of this cute design; I chose an orange napkin with pink rickrack. Any fabric weight will work well; iron with spray starch before folding. After folding, gently press for a tailored look or leave as is for a more casual look.

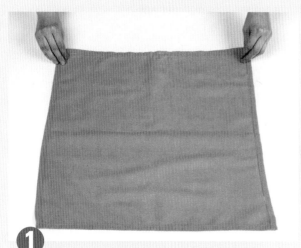

1 Lay the napkin out as a square, with the finished side facing down and the seamed edges facing up.

2 Fold the lower edge up to the upper edge, forming a rectangle.

3 Fold the left edge over to the right edge, forming a square.

4 Rotate the napkin so that it's laid out as a diamond, with the loose points at the bottom. Fold the top two layers of the lower point up to the upper point, so that the trim shows around the entire diamond.

5 Fold the top layer of the upper point down toward the lower point, just far enough to leave about 1 inch (2.5 cm) of the bottom of the diamond exposed.

6 Fold the next layer of the upper point down toward the lower point, just far enough to leave about 1 inch (2.5 cm) of the previous layer exposed.

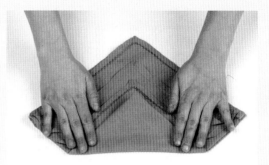

7 Fold the last layer of the upper point down toward the lower point, just far enough to leave about 1 inch (2.5 cm) of the previous layer exposed.

8 Flip the napkin over, keeping the large point down. Fold the left and right sides in at a slight downward angle, overlapping them.

9 Flip the napkin over again and arrange it with the points down.

#23 Hobo Sack

When you want to bundle up a little party favor for your guests, this fold is a great way to do it. The loose, easygoing form of this fold means it will work with any color or pattern in any fabric weight; I chose a red and white checked napkin. I used a wooden clothespin to hold it closed, but you could tie the top with ribbon instead. Iron napkins with spray starch before folding. Have one clothespin, or a 20-inch (50 cm) length of ribbon, and one favor ready for each.

1 Lay the napkin out as a square, with the finished side facing down and the seamed edges facing up.

2 Fold in the lower left and lower right corners, using a little more than one-third the width of the napkin on each side.

3 Fold in the upper left and upper right corners, using a little more than one-third the width of the napkin on each side. Place a favor in the center of the napkin.

4 Gather together the upper and lower flat edges.

5 Holding the upper and lower edges together, add the right flat edge to the gathered edges.

6 Holding the upper, lower and right edges together, add the left flat edge to the gathered edges.

7 Secure all four sides at the top with a clothespin or a ribbon. Arrange the corners of the sack as necessary for the best presentation.

#**24** Liner

You could use this fold for napkins at each place, of course, but its flat form also makes it great for stacking between plates at a buffet table or for lining bread baskets. The Liner fold works with any color or pattern in any fabric weight; here, I chose a solid dark gold napkin. Iron napkins with spray starch before folding. After folding, gently press for a tailored look or leave as is for a more casual look.

1 Lay the napkin out as a square, with the finished side facing down and the seamed edges facing up.

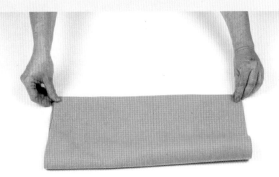

2 Fold the upper edge down to the lower edge, forming a horizontal rectangle.

3 Fold the right edge over to the left edge, forming a square.

4 Fold the top layer of the left edge back toward the right edge, using one-third the width of the napkin.

5 Fold the newly created middle fold over just beyond the right edge, forming a vertical rectangle atop the napkin.

6 Fold the left edge halfway to the vertical rectangle.

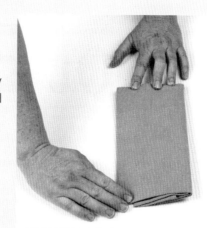

7 Fold the left edge over just beyond the right edge.

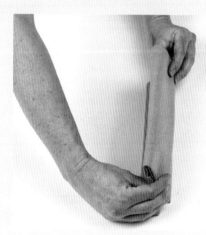

8 Flip the napkin over, keeping the same loose edges down.

9 If necessary, adjust the napkin so that all three layers show.

#25 Loot Bag

Who doesn't like loot? I sure do! This easy napkin fold can hold a party favor or it can be the party favor: fill it with candy that suits your party theme, or even chocolate coins. It works with any color or pattern in any fabric weight; here, I used a red bandana tied with twine (see opposite for a black skull-and-crossbones version). Iron napkins with spray starch before folding. Prepare a 12-inch (30 cm) length of twine or ribbon for each napkin tie or, if you will be tying a bow, prepare a 20-inch (50 cm) length.

1 Lay the napkin out as a square, with the finished side facing down and the seamed edges facing up.

2 Lift the lower right and lower left corners and pinch them together above the napkin.

3 Add the upper left and upper right corners, holding them together above the napkin, forming a bag with four soft points.

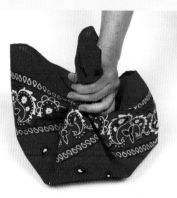

4 Holding the points together, tie twine or ribbon a few inches below the tips, securing the bag.

5 Arrange the corners of the loot bag as necessary for the best presentation.

#26 Parasol

This perky parasol is so showy, yet so easy to fold. I chose a fresh-looking green striped napkin tied with a green organza ribbon, but you could use any striped or patterned medium-weight fabric and any coordinating ribbon. As an alternative to ribbon, try jute or yarn for a rustic look, or simply pull the end through a napkin ring. For crisp results, iron napkins with plenty of spray starch before you get started. Prepare a 20-inch (50 cm) length of ribbon for each napkin.

1 Lay the napkin out as a square, with the finished side facing down and the seamed edges facing up.

2 Fold the lower edge of the napkin up about 1½ inches (4 cm).

3 Fold the lower edge under about 1½ inches (4 cm), aligning the lower edges.

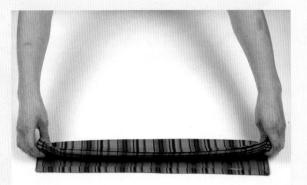

4 Continue folding the lower edge over and under in 1½-inch (4 cm) bands, accordion-style, until you reach the top of the napkin.

5 Place one hand in the center of the napkin and use the other hand to fold it in half lengthwise.

6 Wrap a ribbon around the napkin about 2 inches (5 cm) from the folded side.

7 Turn the napkin so that the pleats are facing up and tie the ribbon into a tight bow.

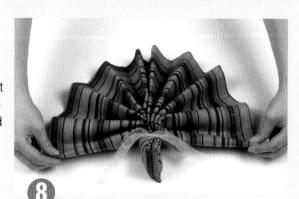

8 Fan out the top of the napkin.

#**27** Placemat

This tidy fold makes a small square placemat suitable for use under a salad, luncheon or dessert plate. With oversized napkins, you can create a placemat large enough for a dinner plate. The underside of the napkin will show in the finished fold, so choose a fabric that's pretty on both sides, like the pastel striped napkin here. Any fabric weight works with this fold. Iron napkins with spray starch before folding. After folding, gently press for a tailored look or leave as is for a more casual look.

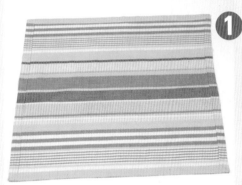

1 Lay the napkin out as a square, with the finished side facing down and the seamed edges facing up.

2 Fold the lower left corner up to the center of the napkin.

3 Fold the lower right corner up to the center.

4 Fold the upper left corner down to the center.

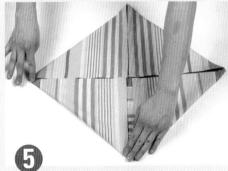

5 Fold the upper right corner down to the center.

6 Flip the fold over, arranging it as a square. Fold the lower right corner up to the center.

7 Fold the lower left corner up to the center.

8 Fold the upper left corner down to the center.

9 Fold the upper right corner down to the center.

10 Flip the napkin over, arranging it as a square. Working in the upper left quadrant, fold the point from the center of the square back to the upper left corner, forming a triangle.

11 Repeat in the remaining three quadrants, folding each point from the center of the square back to the outside corner.

#**28** Pleat

This casual napkin fold results in a tall design with a pleat running down the middle. It works well with any fabric weight. Use a solid or striped napkin, such as the bright red one I used here. Napkins with stripes can have a different look depending on whether you start with the stripes running vertically or horizontally. The fold would also be fun with napkins that have a contrasting reverse side, since the pleat will show a narrow band of the napkin's underside. Iron the napkins with spray starch before folding. After folding, gently press them for a tailored look or leave as is for a more casual look.

1 Lay the napkin out as a square, with the finished side facing down and the seamed edges facing up.

2 Fold the lower edge up about 3½ inches (8.5 cm), forming a horizontal band at the bottom of the napkin.

3 Continue folding the napkin up the same amount and in the same direction, folding about three more times, until you get to the upper edge of the napkin.

4 Flip the napkin over. Lift the top layer of the upper edge and fold the seamed portion back about ½ to ¾ inch (1 to 2 cm). Fold it in the same direction one more time, creating a narrow band that shows the reverse side of the fabric.

6 Arrange the napkin as a vertical rectangle.

5 Pick the napkin up from the center and fold it in half lengthwise.

#29 Pocket

A pocket filled with flatware is the perfect presentation for picnics and casual parties. After placing utensils in each pocket, you can even tie it with twine or ribbon and stack the filled napkins in a basket for picking up at the end of a buffet line. To play up the casual country feel of this fold, I used a blue and white checked napkin, but any fabric weight in any color or pattern will work. Iron napkins with spray starch before folding. After folding, gently press for a tailored look or leave as is for a more casual look.

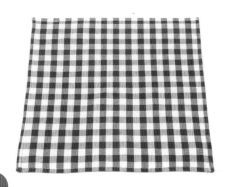

1 Lay the napkin out as a square, with the finished side facing down and the seamed edges facing up.

2 Fold the lower edge up about 3 inches (7.5 cm), forming a horizontal band at the bottom of the napkin.

3 Fold the upper edge down to meet the edge of the previous fold.

4 Flip the napkin over, keeping the same sides up and down. Fold the right edge in to the vertical centerline of the napkin.

5 Fold the left edge in to the vertical centerline.

6 Fold the left edge over to the right edge.

7 Arrange the napkin with the larger rectangle at the bottom.

8 Slide the silverware for each place setting into the pocket.

#30 Pope's Hat

This elegantly easy fold can grace the most formal tables. It looks great in classic white or any other solid-color medium- to heavyweight fabric. Here, I chose a rust red napkin with faint brocade stripes. The simplicity of the Pope's Hat makes it a great choice for embellishment with a decorative item, such as the gold star shown at the bottom of page 79. Iron napkins with spray starch before folding. After folding, gently press for a tailored look.

1 Lay the napkin out as a diamond, with the finished side facing down and the seamed edges facing up.

2 Fold the upper point down to the lower point, forming a triangle.

3 Fold the left point down to the lower point, aligning the edges at the lower left side.

4 Fold the right point down to the lower point, forming a diamond.

5 Fold the top quarter of the diamond under, creating a flat edge at the top of the napkin.

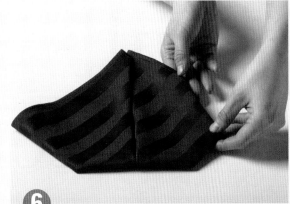

6 Fold the left point underneath the napkin to meet the vertical centerline, forming a vertical edge on the left side.

7 Fold the right point underneath the napkin to meet the vertical centerline, forming a vertical edge on the right side. Gently pull apart the two lower points to expose the middle point. Arrange the napkin on a plate with the points facing up.

#31 Pull-Through

This simple fold is designed for a napkin ring. Its looseness lends it to casual entertaining, as does the blue and white checked napkin I used here. Any napkin ring will work; choose something that complements your napkins and theme. This design works with any color or pattern in any fabric weight. Iron napkins with spray starch before folding.

1 Lay the napkin out as a square, with the finished side facing down and the seamed edges facing up.

2 Fold the lower right corner up toward the upper left corner, positioning it slightly above and to the right of the upper left corner, forming two offset triangles.

3 Fold the upper right corner down toward the lower left corner, positioning it slightly above and to the left of the lower left corner.

4 Holding the point at the center of the right side of the napkin, fold the upper half of the napkin down over the lower half, aligning the layers at the lower right edge.

5 Pull the right point of the napkin through a napkin ring, positioning the ring halfway up the napkin.

6 Arrange the napkin with the tip pointing down.

#32 Ring Roll

This quick and easy roll is perfect for use with napkin rings, and it works with any fabric weight, color and pattern. Here, I used a silky brown napkin paired with a brass rope napkin ring. Iron napkins before folding — there's no need to use spray starch.

1 Lay the napkin out as a square, with the finished side facing down and the seamed edges facing up.

2 Fold the right edge over to the left edge, forming a vertical rectangle.

3 Fold the lower edge up to the upper edge, forming a square.

4 Beginning at the upper edge, loosely roll the napkin down to the lower edge.

6 Arrange the napkin roll seam side down, adjusting the ring as necessary.

5 With the folded edges at the top of the roll and the loose edges at the bottom, slide a napkin ring onto the roll, positioning the ring at the middle of the roll.

#33 Rocket

Talk about dramatic: you'll create instant height on your table with this upright fold. It works with any solid-color or patterned fabric, such as the yellow-green napkin with bright stripes I chose. To help it stand up, choose a medium- to heavyweight fabric and iron napkins with spray starch before folding to give them extra body.

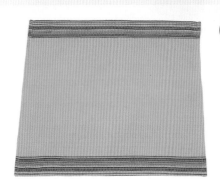

1 Lay the napkin out as a square, with the finished side facing down and the seamed edges facing up.

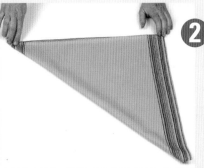

2 Fold the upper right corner down to the lower left corner, forming a triangle.

3 Fold the upper right edge down about 1 inch (2.5 cm), creating a band on the longest side of the triangle.

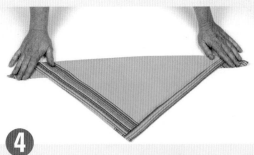

4 Flip the napkin over, positioning the longest side of the triangle at the bottom.

5 Fold the top point down to the middle of the lower edge.

6 Leaving a 1-inch (2.5 cm) band at the top of the napkin, fold the middle point back up.

8 Beginning at the left edge, roll the napkin up all the way to the right point.

7 Fold the left point over toward the right point, using one-third the width of the lower edge and aligning the lower edges.

9 Tuck the right point into the band at the base of the napkin to secure it.

10 Stand the rocket up on its base. Fold the outer layer of the top tip down, forming a downward-pointing triangle.

11 Arrange a rocket upright at each place.

#34 Rosebud

For picnics or buffets, I like placing a basket of these napkins next to the plates. Any fabric weight in any color or pattern works. To play up the rosebud look, choose a solid-color napkin that complements the occasion (red for Valentine's Day, white for a bridal shower, yellow for a birthday party). Or choose a fun floral print, as I did here with a multicolored daisy pattern. Iron napkins with spray starch before folding.

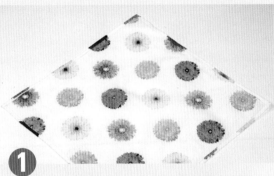

1 Lay the napkin out as a diamond, with the finished side facing down and the seamed edges facing up.

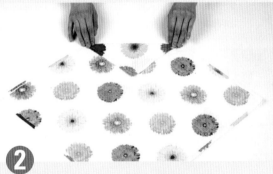

2 Fold the bottom point up about 4 inches (10 cm).

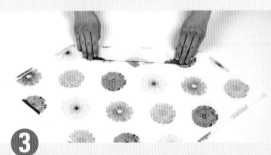

3 Fold the lower edge up almost to the point.

4 Continue folding up six or seven more times, until you reach the top of the napkin.

5 Turn the napkin to a vertical position. Starting at the end closest to you, begin rolling it up.

6 Continue rolling until you reach the top.

7 Tuck the loose point securely into the nearest fold.

8 Stand the rosebud upright on its base and carefully pull layers of napkin up from the center, creating a petal-like effect.

#⓵⓹ Sailboat

This fun, casual design is suitable for either kids or adults. I chose a blue, green and white wavy-striped napkin to play up the nautical theme. The fold will work with solids, patterns or stripes in all fabric weights. Iron napkins with spray starch before folding. After folding, gently press for a tailored look or leave as is for a more casual look.

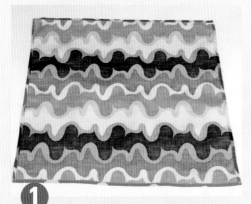

① Lay the napkin out as a square, with the finished side facing down and the seamed edges facing up.

② Fold the upper right point down to the lower left point, forming a triangle.

③ Rotate the triangle so that the longest side is at the top, with the middle point down.

④ Holding the bottom point with your right hand, use your left hand to fold the left point up until the edges run up the vertical centerline of the napkin.

5 Holding the bottom point with your left hand, use your right hand to fold the right point up until the edges run up the vertical centerline of the napkin.

6 Fold the upper left tip of the napkin down so that the fold is flush with the fold beneath it and the right edges align in the center of the napkin.

7 Fold the upper right tip of the napkin down so that the fold is flush with the fold beneath it and the left edges align in the center of the napkin.

8 Using the top third of the napkin, fold the upper edge down at a slight angle, giving the boat a jaunty look.

#36 Shield

This easy fold can go formal with an elegant solid-colored napkin or fun with a whimsical patterned fabric, such as the white, green and yellow lemon napkin I used. It works best with medium- to heavyweight fabric. Iron with spray starch before folding. After folding, gently press for a tailored look or leave as is for a casual look. Tuck a place card or a small favor into the pointed pocket, if you like.

1 Lay the napkin out as a square, with the finished side facing down and the seamed edges facing up.

2 Fold the lower edge up to the upper edge, forming a horizontal rectangle.

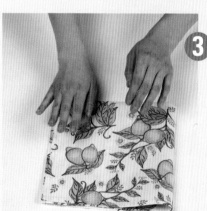

3 Fold the left edge over to the right edge, forming a square.

4 Fold the lower left corner just past the center of the napkin.

5 Flip the napkin over, positioning it with the new flat side at the bottom. Fold the left and right sides in, overlapping them to create a shield shape with a flat bottom.

6 Flip the napkin back over and arrange it with the points up.

#37 Simple Upright

It doesn't get any easier than this. Dress up a plain napkin with a decal or sticker, then use a simple fold to show it off. (Arts and crafts stores, such as Michaels, offer a variety of decals and stencils that can add style to your table linens.) You can also leave the embellishment off and simply lean a place card against the napkin fold. The Simple Upright fold works with any color or pattern in any fabric weight. Here, I used a pale yellow napkin with a gold bird decal. Iron napkins with spray starch before folding. Lightly press after folding, taking care to avoid ironing any decorations.

1 Lay the napkin out as a square, with the finished side facing up and the seamed edges facing down. Add a decal near the lower edge of the napkin, just to the left of the vertical centerline.

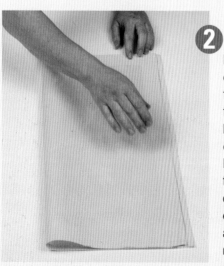

2 Flip the napkin over so that the finished side is facing down, keeping the decal at the lower edge. Fold the left edge over to the right edge, forming a vertical rectangle.

3 Fold the left edge over to the right edge again, forming a narrower rectangle with the decal showing just above the lower edge.

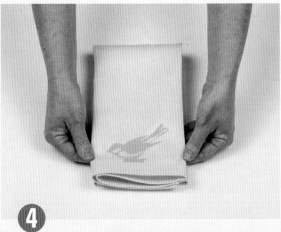

4 Fold the upper edge underneath the napkin to meet the lower edge.

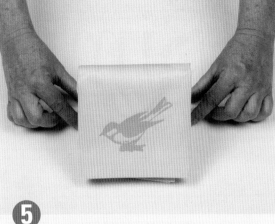

5 Again fold the upper edge underneath the napkin to meet the lower edge, forming a small square. Separate the top and bottom layers to stand the napkin upright.

#38 Simplicity

Show off napkins with lace edges to their best advantage with this elegant fold, in which two decorative edges grace the entire front length. It's a lovely design for any casual or formal occasion. Any fabric weight works. I chose an ivory napkin with an embroidered border. Iron napkins with spray starch before folding. After folding, gently press for a tailored look or leave as is for a more casual look.

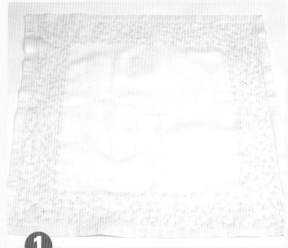

1 Lay the napkin out as a square, with the finished side facing down and the seamed edges facing up.

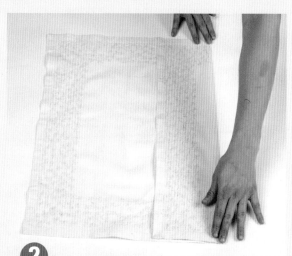

2 Fold the left edge in to the vertical centerline of the napkin.

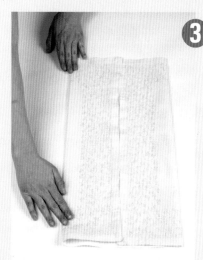

3 Fold the right edge in to the vertical centerline.

4 Flip the napkin over, leaving it as a vertical rectangle. Fold the left edge in to the vertical centerline.

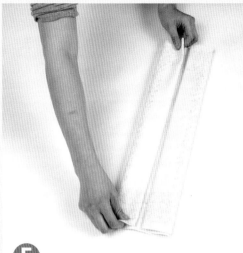

5 Fold the right edge in to the vertical centerline.

6 Fold the lower edge up to the upper edge. Arrange the napkin with the loose edges at the bottom.

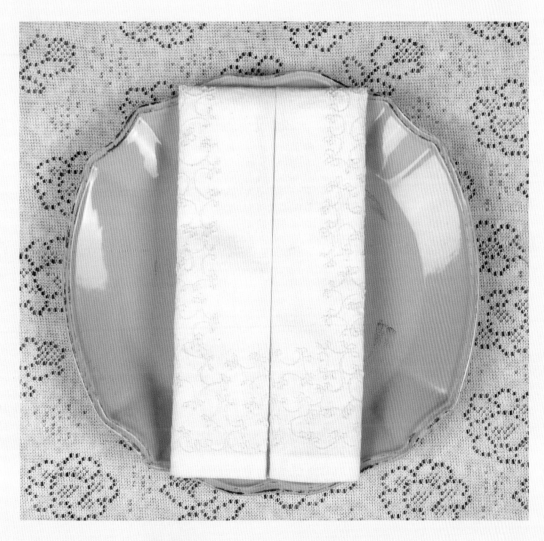

#39 Simply Skinny

Present this simple fold plainly, as shown here, pull it through a napkin ring or dress it up with a decorative clip. Here, I chose a solid yellow napkin, but the fold will be pretty with any color or pattern in any fabric weight. Iron napkins with spray starch before folding. After folding, gently press for a tailored look or leave as is for a more casual look.

1 Lay the napkin out as a square, with the finished side facing down and the seamed edges facing up.

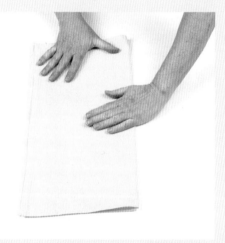

2 Fold the left edge over to the right edge, forming a vertical rectangle.

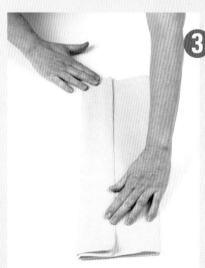

3 Fold the right edge in toward the left edge, using one-third the width of the napkin.

4 Fold the left edge over to the right edge, forming a skinny vertical rectangle.

5 Fold the lower edge up to the upper edge.

6 Arrange the napkin with the loose edges at the bottom.

#40 Single Wing

Simple and elegant, this design works for any sit-down meal, from fancy to casual. Choose a muted solid napkin for more elegant meals or any color or pattern for more festive ones. I used a tan napkin with a wide white border, which is shown off nicely in the finished fold. Medium- to heavyweight fabric works best for this fold, which needs the bulk to stand up successfully. To stiffen the fabric further, starch and iron napkins well before folding.

1 Lay the napkin out as a square, with the finished side facing up and the seamed edges facing down.

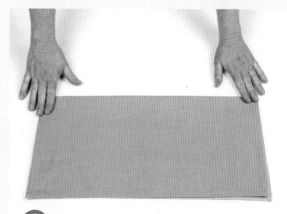

2 Fold the lower edge up to the upper edge, forming a horizontal rectangle.

3 Fold the right edge over to the left edge, forming a square.

4 Fold the upper left corner down to the lower right corner, forming a triangle.

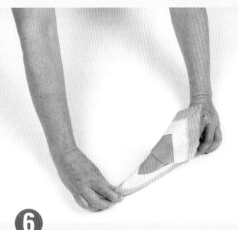

5 Working with the top two layers of fabric, fold the lower right corner back toward the upper left corner, forming a small square atop the napkin fold.

6 Slide the upper right and lower left points toward each other, lifting the middle of the napkin to stand it upright.

7 Arrange the napkin on an angle at each place.

#41 The Standard

This is the napkin fold of the typical family dinner. Make it special by using starched and ironed cloth napkins, such as the beige hemstitched napkin shown here. Any color or pattern and any fabric weight will work. After folding, gently press for a tailored look or leave as is for a more casual look. Place the finished napkin atop each plate, if you like.

1 Lay the napkin out as a square, with the finished side facing down and the seamed edges facing up.

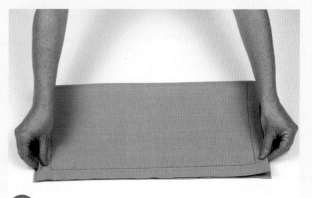

2 Fold the lower edge up to the upper edge, forming a horizontal rectangle.

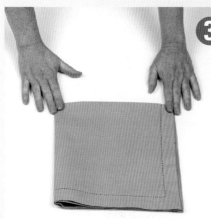

3 Fold the right edge over to the left edge, forming a square.

4 Flip the napkin over, keeping the same edges at the top and bottom. Fold the right edge over to the left edge.

5 Arrange the napkin with the loose edges at the right and lower edges.

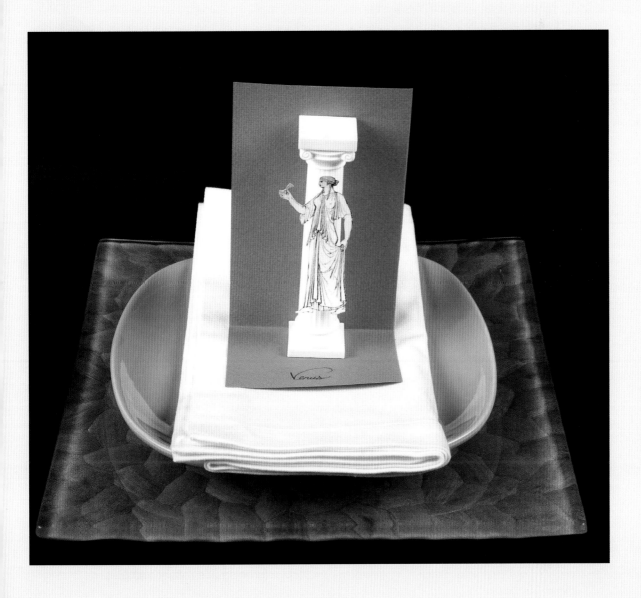

#42 Three Flags

Easy and elegant, this fold can be used with any fabric weight in any color or pattern. I chose a solid medium blue napkin. Iron napkins with spray starch before folding, and press again after folding. This fold can be draped over the back of each chair or over the edge of the table at each place setting.

1 Lay the napkin out as a square, with the finished side facing down and the seamed edges facing up.

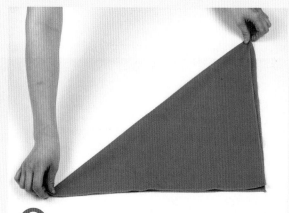

2 Fold the lower right corner up to the upper left corner, forming a triangle.

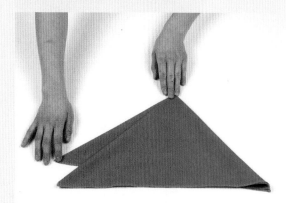

3 Fold the lower left point up just above and to the left of the upper right point, forming two smaller offset triangles.

4 Fold the left point over toward the right points, placing it just above and to the left of them, forming three smaller offset triangles.

5 Tuck the left side of the top triangle under the napkin to form a narrower stack of triangles.

6 Arrange the napkin fold with the three points down.

#43 Three-Fold

This fold really shows off napkins with wide decorative borders, such as this gorgeous Provence-inspired yellow napkin with red flowers. The finished napkin fold has three triangles, hence the name. Any fabric weight will work, although thicker napkins will need to be pressed after folding to lie flat. Iron napkins with spray starch before folding.

1 Lay the napkin out as a square, with the finished side facing down and the seamed edges facing up.

2 Fold the right edge over to the left edge, forming a vertical rectangle.

3 Fold the lower edge up to the upper edge, forming a square.

4 Fold the upper left point down to the lower right point, forming a triangle.

5 Flip the napkin over and fold the center point over to touch the middle of the opposite side. Press as necessary and arrange vertically.

#44 Tie One On

This simple napkin fold isn't necessarily one you'll use at each place setting, but it's perfect for dressing up any serving piece with a handle, from wicker baskets to trays to beer steins. It works well with any color or pattern in any fabric weight, and will even work with slightly smaller luncheon napkins. I used a white napkin with a bright daisy pattern. Iron napkins with spray starch before folding.

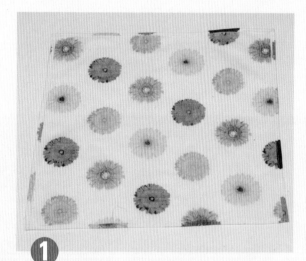

1 Lay the napkin out as a square, with the finished side facing down and the seamed edges facing up.

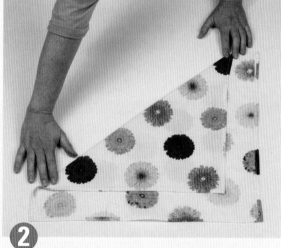

2 Fold the lower right corner up toward the upper left corner, leaving 2 to 3 inches (5 to 7.5 cm) of the bottom layer exposed.

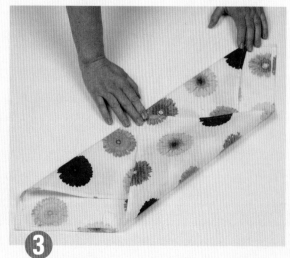

3 Fold the upper left point down to the middle of the lower right edge.

4 Fold the upper left edge down to the lower right edge.

5 Gripping the upper left and lower right sides together to make a narrow strip, pick up the napkin.

6 Lace one end of the napkin through the handle of a serving piece.

7 Tie the napkin into a single knot.

8 Arrange the serving piece to show off the tied handle.

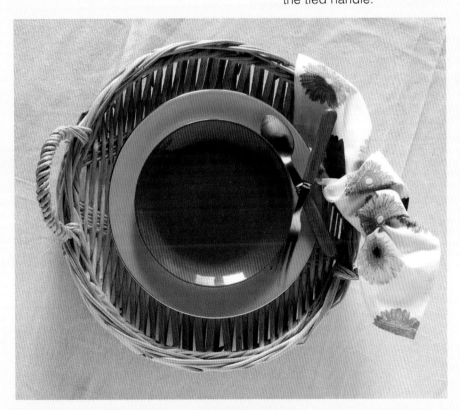

#45 Tray Roll

This roll makes a neat way to bundle utensils and napkins together, which is especially handy if you're placing them on a tray for a meal away from the table. These rolls are also great placed at the end of a buffet line; in that case, use lengths of raffia or ribbon to hold them together. Here, I chose a red and green striped tea towel that would be perfect for Christmas, but this rolled-up design works well with any color or pattern in any fabric weight. Iron tea towels or napkins with spray starch before folding.

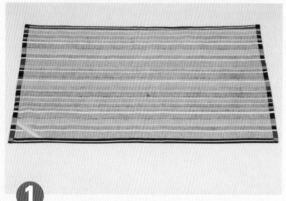

1 Lay the napkin out flat, with the finished side facing down and the seamed edges facing up.

2 Fold the lower edge up toward the upper edge, using one-third the height of the napkin.

3 Fold the upper edge down to the lower edge, forming a narrow horizontal rectangle.

4 Place utensils on top of the napkin, about one-quarter of the way in from the right edge. Align the handles of the utensils just above the lower edge of the napkin.

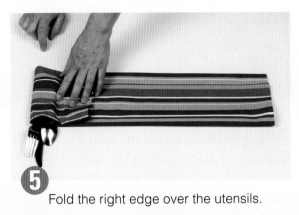

5 Fold the right edge over the utensils.

6 Starting from the right edge, roll up utensils until you reach the end of the napkin.

7 Arrange utensils at each place. For buffets, tie rolls closed with raffia or ribbon.

#46 Trifold

I used a silky brown napkin for this simple fold, which shows off, in its three layers, the lustrous sheen of the fabric. This fold can be left as is or gathered with the use of a napkin ring, as in the photo on the bottom of page 111. Use any fabric weight in any color or pattern. This fold looks best if the napkins are ironed with spray starch before folding; after folding, gently press for a tailored look or leave as is for a more casual look.

1

Lay the napkin out as a square, with the finished side facing down and the seamed edges facing up.

2

Fold the lower edge up toward the upper edge, using one-third the height of the napkin.

3

Fold the upper edge down to the lower edge, forming a horizontal rectangle.

4 Fold the left edge about 2 inches (5 cm) to the right, forming a vertical band.

5 Pick up the vertical band and fold another vertical band under it and offset to the right of the original band.

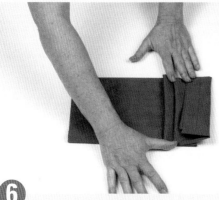

6 Pick up both vertical bands and fold a third vertical band under them and offset to the right of the second band.

7 Fold the right edge over to meet the closest vertical band.

8 Flip the napkin over.

9 Arrange the napkin with the bands at the top.

#**47** Tulip

Like a few other designs in this book, the Tulip fold can be arranged flat at each place or stand upright, bringing height to your place settings. To help it stand up, choose a medium- to heavyweight fabric and lightly starch it before ironing. I chose a multicolored tropical flower print. Try it with a solid-color napkin for a formal dinner or, for a more casual table, with any pattern that coordinates with your theme.

1 Lay the napkin out as a diamond, with the finished side facing down and the seamed edges facing up.

2 Fold the upper point down to the lower point, forming a triangle.

3 Fold the right point down to the lower point.

4 Fold the left point down to the lower point, forming a diamond.

5 Flip the napkin over, keeping the same point up.

6 Fold the upper point down toward the lower point, leaving about 2 inches (5 cm) of the bottom layer showing.

7 Flip the napkin over again, keeping the same point down. Fold the left side over toward the right side, using about one-third the width of the napkin.

8 Fold the right side over to the left edge, overlapping the previous fold.

9 Tuck the tip of the fold under the top layer of the previous fold to secure it.

10 Flip the napkin over and arrange it with the point up.

11 Alternatively, open up the base and arrange the napkin standing upright.

#48 Two Points

This easy fold can take on a very formal appearance when done with a white napkin, or can be more festive when a color or pattern is used. I like using napkins with a decorative border, such as this beige napkin with white edging, to play up the fold's two points. Any fabric weight will work. Iron napkins with spray starch before folding. After folding, gently press for a tailored look or leave as is for a more casual look.

1 Lay the napkin out as a diamond, with the finished side facing down and the seamed edges facing up.

2 Fold the lower point up toward the upper point, leaving about 2 inches (5 cm) of the bottom layer showing.

3 Flip the napkin over, keeping the same point up. Holding the middle of the lower edge with your right hand, use your left hand to fold the left point up toward the upper point, so that the inner edge of the fold creates a vertical centerline.

4 Fold the right point up toward the upper point until the inner edge of the fold meets the vertical centerline.

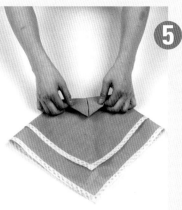

5 Flip the napkin over, keeping the same points up and down. Fold the lower point up about 2 inches (5 cm).

6 Flip the napkin over again, keeping the same flat edge down. Fold the lower left diagonal edge over to meet the vertical centerline.

7 Fold the lower right diagonal edge over to meet the vertical centerline.

8 Flip the napkin over and arrange it with the flat edge up.

#49 Two Tails

This elegant, easy presentation will work with any fabric weight, in any color or pattern; white is the most formal-looking. Here, I used a warm orange linen hemstitched napkin. Dress it up with a tassel or other decorative object, if you like (as in the photo on the bottom of page 117). Iron napkins with spray starch before folding. After folding, gently press for a more tailored look or leave as is for more casual results.

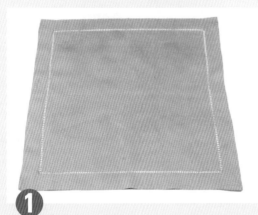

1 Lay the napkin out as a square, with the finished side facing down and the seamed edges facing up.

2 Fold the upper left point down to the lower right point, forming a triangle.

3 Fold the left point over to the lower right point, aligning the lower edges.

4 Fold the upper right point down to the lower right point, forming a square.

5 Fold the upper left corner under the napkin toward the lower right corner, using one-third the length of the diagonal of the square.

6 Fold the left edge over to meet the diagonal centerline (or past it for smaller plates).

7 Fold the upper edge over to meet the diagonal centerline (or past it for smaller plates).

8 Flip the napkin over. Arrange it on the plate with the tips pointing up or down.

#**50** Vase

This fold makes a cute container for a silk flower at each place setting (you could use a fresh flower, but keep in mind that it won't be in water and add it at the last minute so it doesn't wilt). Slightly smaller napkins work better than larger ones. Any fabric weight will do. Choose a color and pattern that suits the occasion; fringed or lacy edges will be shown off to their best advantage in this design. I used a lavender and white checked napkin with a fringed edge. Iron napkins with spray starch before folding. After folding, gently press for a tailored look or leave as is for a more casual look.

1 Lay the napkin out as a diamond, with the finished side facing down and the seamed edges facing up.

2 Fold the lower corner up to the upper corner, forming a triangle.

3 Fold the left point up to the upper point.

4 Fold the right point up to the upper point, forming a diamond.

5 Fold the lower left edge over to the vertical centerline.

6 Fold the lower right edge over to the vertical centerline, forming a kite shape.

7 Working with the top layer only, fold the upper left point down.

8 Working with the top layer only, fold the upper right point down.

9 Flip the napkin over. Fold the top point down, aligning the top edge with the folded layers beneath.

Intermediate Napkin Folds

#**51** Basket

Perfect for any spring or summertime brunch or lunch, especially one held outside on the patio, the Basket fold can be presented on its own or with a place card, flower or sprig of herbs tucked into one of its many folds. Choose a cloth napkin in any pattern or color that coordinates with your party theme. I chose a bright yellow patterned napkin with a solid border, which shows up nicely in the finished fold. Be sure to use napkins that are pretty on both sides, as both sides will be visible in the finished design.

1 Lay the napkin out as a diamond, with the finished side facing up and the seamed edges facing down.

2 Fold the lower left edge up to the upper right edge, forming a rectangle.

3 Fold the lower right edge up to the upper left edge, forming a diamond.

4 Tuck the top layer of the upper point under to meet the inside of the lower point.

5 The napkin will now have a visible horizontal centerline.

6 Tuck the next layer of the upper point under just far enough to leave a 1-inch (2.5 cm) band above the horizontal centerline.

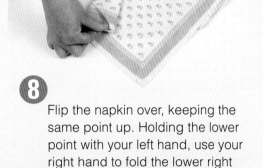

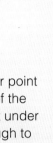 **7** Fold the next layer of the upper point over so that the finished side of the fabric shows, tucking the point under the previous layer just far enough to leave a 1-inch (2.5 cm) band above the previous band.

8 Flip the napkin over, keeping the same point up. Holding the lower point with your left hand, use your right hand to fold the lower right edge in at an angle, about two-thirds of the way to the vertical centerline.

9 Holding the lower point with your right hand, use your left hand to fold the lower left edge in at an angle, about two-thirds of the way to the vertical centerline.

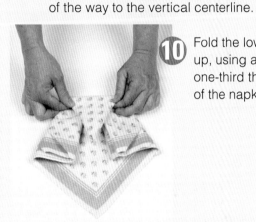

10 Fold the lower tip up, using about one-third the height of the napkin.

11 Flip the napkin over and arrange pointed side up at each place.

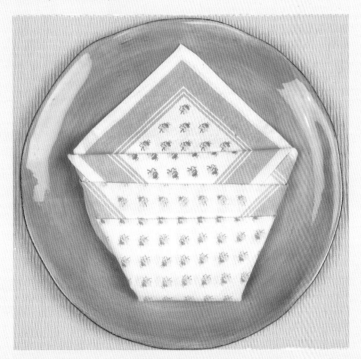

#52 Bunny

What could be more fitting for Easter dinner or a springtime brunch than this cute fellow placed atop each plate? Add candy or button eyes to the finished Bunny fold to make it even more recognizable. Any color or pattern will do; for springtime parties, think white or solid pastels, such as the pale yellow napkin I used here. It's best to use a lightweight fabric so that the ears stay folded. Iron napkins with spray starch before folding, and press gently after folding.

1 Lay the napkin out as a square, with the finished side facing down and the seamed edges facing up.

2 Fold the lower edge up to the horizontal centerline of the napkin.

3 Fold the upper edge down to the horizontal centerline.

4 Fold the lower edge up to the upper edge, forming a thin horizontal rectangle.

5 Holding the middle of the lower edge in place with your left hand, use your right hand to fold the lower edge of the right half up to the vertical centerline of the napkin.

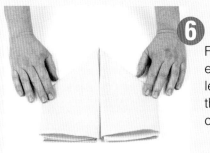

6 Fold the lower edge of the left half up to the vertical centerline.

7 Fold the upper right corner down, forming a triangle on the right side.

8 Fold the upper left corner down, forming a diamond.

9 Fold the upper right edge of the diamond in to meet the vertical centerline.

10 Fold the upper left edge of the diamond in to meet the vertical centerline.

11 Flip the napkin over. Arrange at each place with ears up.

#53 Cabbage Rose

This gorgeous fold is easier than it looks; once you get the hang of it, you'll be able to create these quickly. Because this design has a pretty, feminine, floral look, try it for any occasion that's girls-only or has a female guest of honor. Use a medium-weight fabric, lightly starched and ironed, in any color or pattern. The Cabbage Rose design gives you a great way to present a flower blossom, a small favor or even a roll, muffin or scone at each place.

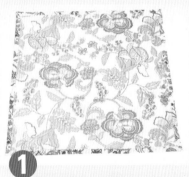

1 Lay the napkin out as a square, with the finished side facing down and the seamed edges facing up.

2 Fold the lower left and right corners in to the center of the napkin.

3 Fold the upper left and right corners in to the center of the napkin, forming a diamond.

4 Fold the right point in to the center of the napkin.

5 Fold the left point in to the center of the napkin.

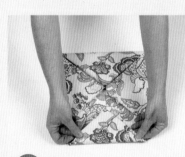

6 Fold the upper and lower points in to the center of the napkin, forming a square.

7 Fold the lower left and right corners in to the center of the napkin.

8 Fold the upper left and right corners in to the center of the napkin, forming a diamond.

9 Flip the diamond over and arrange it as a square. Fold the upper right corner in to the center of the napkin.

10 Fold the remaining three corners in to the center of the napkin, forming a diamond.

11 Holding the center of the diamond steady with your left hand, use your right hand to reach underneath the upper point and find the center point beneath it. Gently pull that point out to form a petal.

12 Repeat on the remaining three points. Holding the center of the diamond steady with one hand, use the other hand to reach underneath each point and find the center point beneath it. Gently pull each center point out to form a petal.

13 Holding the center of the napkin steady with your right hand, use your left hand to reach underneath the upper left edge and find the center point beneath it. Gently pull that point out and up, forming a petal.

14 Repeat on the remaining three edges. Holding the center of the napkin steady with one hand, use the other hand to reach underneath each edge and find the center point beneath it. Gently pull each center point out and up to form a petal. Arrange a cabbage rose at each place.

#54 Clown Hat

You don't have to be a kid to get a kick out of this cute fold. While it can be left flat on the plate, it's a lot more fun when presented standing up, so choose a medium- to heavyweight fabric that will stay upright. It also helps to iron the napkins with spray starch before folding them. This design is most festive with a fun patterned fabric, like the green napkin with big brown polka dots I used here. Surprise your guests by hiding a little something underneath each napkin.

1 Lay the napkin out as a square, with the finished side facing down and the seamed edges facing up.

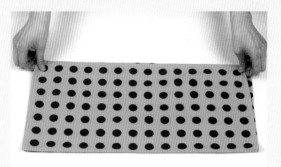

2 Fold the upper edge down to the lower edge, forming a horizontal rectangle.

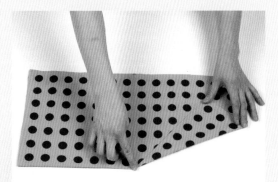

3 Holding the middle of the upper edge with your right hand, use your left hand to fold the upper left corner down, creating a slim triangle with a roughly 3-inch (7.5 cm) base atop the napkin. Smooth the fold.

4 Continuing to hold the middle of the upper edge with your right hand, pick up the newly folded upper left edge and fold it over again, making the fold the same width as the previous one.

5 Fold the triangle over again so that the right edge meets the vertical centerline.

6 Fold two more times, heading toward the other end of the napkin.

7 Fold the triangle one last time to reach the end of the napkin, aligning the end of the napkin with the edge of the triangle.

8 Rotate the napkin so that the point is facing you.

9 Reach into the base of the triangle and turn the bottom third inside out, forming a cone.

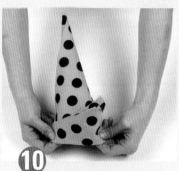

10 Open the cone up so that it stands upright. Stand a clown hat upright at each place and arrange the points as necessary.

#55 Cowl

The Cowl fold is simple and elegant, and it has a little opening that could hold a small favor or a piece of candy. Try it with a solid blue, white or aqua napkin (as I used here) for a party with a Greek theme. For any other sit-down dinner party, select a fabric in a color or pattern that complements your theme and setting. This fold works best with large lightweight napkins; starch and press them before you begin.

1 Lay the napkin out as a square, with the finished side facing down and the seamed edges facing up.

2 Fold the upper edge down toward the lower edge, using one-third the height of the napkin.

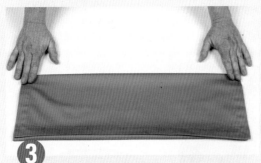

3 Fold the lower edge up to the upper edge, forming a horizontal rectangle.

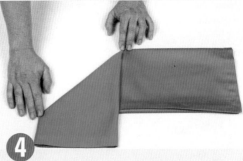

4 Holding the middle of the lower edge with your left hand, use your right hand to fold the right half of the lower edge up almost to the vertical centerline of the napkin.

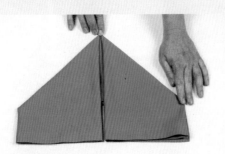

5 Fold the left half of the lower edge up almost to the vertical centerline, leaving a small gap in the middle.

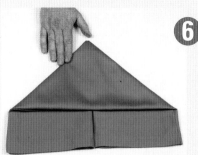

6 Flip the napkin over, keeping the point down and the tails up.

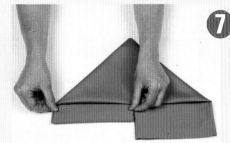

7 Fold the upper edge of the right tail down to almost meet the top of the triangle.

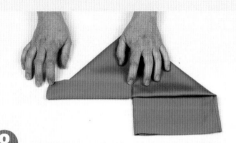

8 Fold the right tail down again, forming a band on top of the right side of the triangle.

9 Fold the upper edge of the left tail down to almost meet the top of the triangle. Fold the left tail down again, forming a band on top of the left side of the triangle.

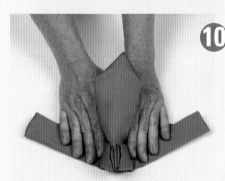

10 Placing one hand atop each band, pull the bands down to meet under the triangle.

11 Arrange the bands parallel to each other, flat on the work surface, with the triangle extending up.

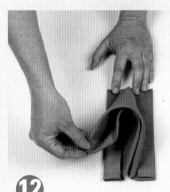

12 Curl the triangle around to one side to form a round opening. Arrange at each place with the opening facing down.

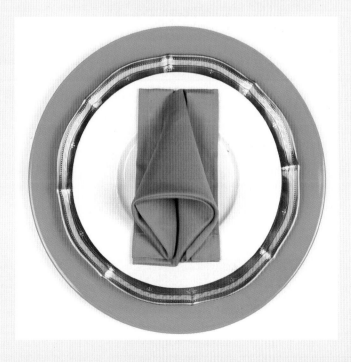

#56 Diagonal

Use double-sided napkins to enjoy the full impact of this fold, which shows off both sides in alternating diagonal bands. I used a brown floral napkin with a coordinating stripe on the reverse side. Any fabric weight will work. Iron napkins with spray starch before folding. After folding, gently press for a tailored look or leave as is for a more casual look.

1 Lay the napkin out as a square, with the finished side facing down and the seamed edges facing up.

2 Fold the lower edge up to the upper edge, forming a horizontal rectangle.

3 Fold the top layer of the upper edge back down, leaving a 2-inch (5 cm) band of fabric showing below the edge.

4 Fold the remaining layer of the top edge down over the newly folded edge, creating an upper band that's the same width as the lower one, about 2 inches (5 cm) tall.

5 Flip the napkin over so that the previous fold is at the lower edge. Fold the lower left corner up to the horizontal centerline, forming a small triangle on top of the napkin.

6 Using the right edge of the triangle as a guide, fold the left side over toward the right side.

7 Fold the upper right corner down to the horizontal centerline, forming a small triangle on top of the napkin.

8 Using the left edge of the triangle as a guide, fold the right side over toward the left side.

9 Fold the lower right corner up to the center of the upper edge, forming a triangle on top of the napkin.

10 Fold the upper left corner down to the center of the lower edge, forming a parallelogram.

11 Flip the napkin over and arrange it horizontally.

#57 Double Envelope

This fun fold makes a lovely base for name tags or party favors. It works best with medium- to heavyweight fabrics, such as this pretty multicolored blue, white and green floral napkin. A portion of the napkin's underside will show in the finished fold, so choose a fabric that's pretty on both sides. Iron with spray starch before folding. After folding, gently press for crisp results. The finished fold works well arranged vertically, horizontally or even diagonally on each plate.

1 Lay the napkin out as a square, with the finished side facing down and the seamed edges facing up.

2 Fold the lower edge up to the upper edge, forming a horizontal rectangle.

3 Fold the left edge over to the right edge, forming a square.

4 Fold the top layer of the upper right corner down to the lower left corner, creating a triangle on top of the square.

5 Fold the top layer of the lower left corner into the center of the napkin, creating a smaller triangle.

6 Fold the top layer of the upper right corner into the center of the napkin, creating another small triangle.

7 Tuck the upper left corner under to the center of the napkin.

8 Tuck the lower right corner under to the center of the napkin.

#58 Double Pleats

This sweet and versatile fold works well with fabric in any weight, color and pattern, resulting in a small diamond shape with two pleats running up the middle. I chose a rusty orange napkin with a small calico print, for a country look. Iron napkins with spray starch before folding. After folding, gently press for a tailored look or leave as is for a more casual look.

1 Lay the napkin out as a square, with the finished side facing down and the seamed edges facing up.

2 Fold the upper edge down toward the lower edge, using one-third the height of the napkin.

3 Fold the lower edge up to the upper edge, forming a horizontal rectangle.

4 Holding the middle of the lower edge with your right hand, use your left hand to fold the left half of the lower edge up to the vertical centerline of the napkin.

5 Fold the right half of the lower edge up to the vertical centerline.

6 Flip the napkin over, keeping the point down and the tails up. Fold the upper edge of the left tail down to meet the top of the triangle.

7 Fold the left tail down again, forming a band on top of the left side of the triangle.

8 Fold the upper edge of the right tail down to meet the top of the triangle. Fold the right tail down again, forming a band on top of the right side of the triangle.

9 Flip the napkin over, keeping the point down. Holding the middle of the upper edge with your right hand, use your left hand to fold the left side down so that the band meets the vertical centerline.

10 Fold the right side down so that the band meets the vertical centerline. Arrange the napkin vertically or horizontally on a plate.

#59 Exploding Envelope

This elaborate-looking fold can be arranged flat at each place or stand upright for an even more dramatic presentation. Choose a medium- to heavyweight fabric and lightly starch and press napkins before you begin folding. Solid colors keep the focus on its striking folded form, so avoid using busy patterns for this design — I chose a bright gold napkin here.

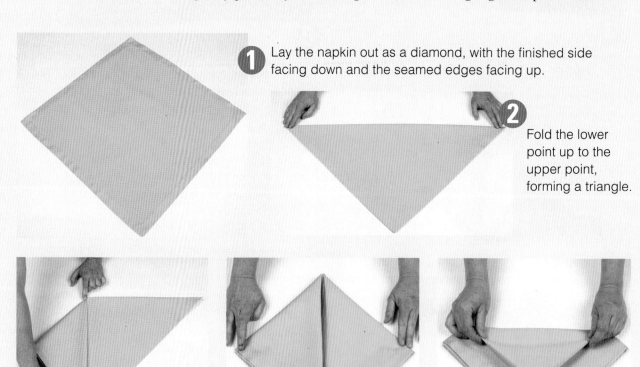

1 Lay the napkin out as a diamond, with the finished side facing down and the seamed edges facing up.

2 Fold the lower point up to the upper point, forming a triangle.

3 Holding the middle of the lower edge with your left hand, use your right hand to fold the right point up to the upper point.

4 Fold the left point up to the upper point, forming a diamond.

5 Fold the lower point up toward the upper point, leaving about 2 inches (5 cm) of the bottom layer showing.

6 Working with the top layer only, fold the center point down to the lower edge of the napkin.

7 Working with the right side of the upper point, fold the top layer down to the lower edge of the napkin, tucking it under the top fold.

8 Working with the left side of the upper point, fold the top layer down to the lower edge of the napkin, tucking it under the top fold.

9 Fold the top layer of the upper point down, tucking it under the previous layer, leaving a small band showing at the top.

10 Flip the napkin over, keeping the same point up. Fold the right point over toward the left, using one-third the width of the napkin and creating a vertical right edge.

11 Fold the left point over toward the right, using one-third the width of the napkin and creating a vertical left edge. Tuck the left point into the pocket at the right to secure it.

12 Flip the napkin over and arrange it with the point up. Alternatively, open up the base and arrange the napkin standing upright.

#**60** Fish

This whimsical napkin fold is fun for kids and adults — think pool party, a seafood menu or even Chinese takeout (the fish is a symbol of abundance in Chinese culture). While any patterned or solid-color fabric will work, I like bright, lively colors for this fold. Use medium- to heavyweight cloth napkins, iron them with spray starch before folding and press gently after folding. Place a button, candy, stone, coin or other decorative element where the eye would be on each napkin.

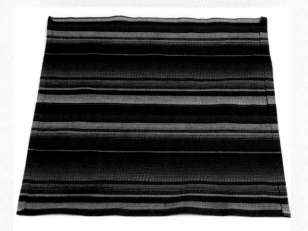

1 Lay the napkin out as a square, with the finished side facing down and the seamed edges facing up.

2 Fold the upper left corner down to the lower right corner, forming a triangle.

3 Turn the triangle so that the widest edge is at the top. Fold the upper edge down to form a 2-inch (5 cm) wide band.

4 Flip the napkin over, keeping the point down.

5 Holding the middle of the upper edge with your right hand, use your left hand to fold the left point down so that the band meets the vertical centerline, leaving a tail at the bottom.

6 Fold the right point down so that the band meets the vertical centerline, leaving a tail at the bottom.

7 Fold the left tail at a 90-degree angle to point out to the left. Fold the right tail at a 90-degree angle to point out to the right. Using an iron, gently press into place.

8 Flip the napkin over. Arrange the fish on a plate, facing right or left. Add a decorative eye, if desired.

#61 Fleur

Arranged in a coffee cup or teacup, this is a lovely fold for serving after-dinner coffee, tea or dessert. Use a slightly smaller napkin that is ironed without starch. Any color or pattern and any fabric weight will work well; I chose a silky purple napkin arranged in a white china coffee cup. For larger latte-style mugs, use a full-size dinner napkin.

1 Lay the napkin out as a square, with the finished side facing down and the seamed edges facing up.

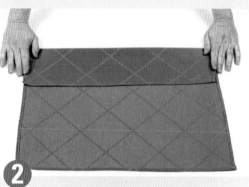

2 Fold the lower edge up to the horizontal centerline of the napkin.

3 Fold the upper edge down to the horizontal centerline.

4 Fold the upper edge down to the lower edge, forming a narrow horizontal rectangle.

5 Fold the right edge over to the left edge, forming a smaller rectangle.

6 Fold the top layer back over to the right, leaving a small overlapped area about three-quarters of the way along the napkin.

7 Fold the right side back over to the left, aligning the right edges.

8 Fold the loose edges in the center of the napkin back over to the right, aligning the left edges. If necessary, fold the end of the right edge back over to the left to align the right edges.

9 Flip the napkin over, arranging the stack of folded edges on the left and the loose end on the right. Fold the right edge over to the left, aligning the right edges.

10 Continue folding accordion-style until napkin is completely folded into a stack.

11 Place napkin in cup with the loose edges facing you. Pull gently from the sides to fan the napkin out.

12 Working with the three folded edges facing you, pull each apart at the top to give the napkin more volume. Arrange a cup at each place with the loose edges facing the center of the table.

#62 Fleur de Lis

There is something elegant and a bit royal about this French-inspired fold, which is why I used a beautiful deep purple napkin. It will work with any color or pattern in any fabric weight. Iron napkins with spray starch before folding. You can lay a finished napkin on each plate or arrange it in a wineglass or water glass.

1 Lay the napkin out as a square, with the finished side facing down and the seamed edges facing up.

2 Fold the upper right corner down to the lower left corner, forming a triangle.

3 Fold the lower right point over to the lower left corner, aligning the lower edges.

4 Fold the upper left point down to the lower left corner, forming a square.

5 Working with the upper left corner, insert your thumbs into the center of the layers and pull the upper layers toward the diagonal centerline, forming a triangle with a 3-inch (7.5 cm) base, with the edges aligned along the diagonal centerline. Smooth flat.

6 Working with the lower right corner, insert your thumbs into the center of the layers and pull the upper layers toward the diagonal centerline, forming a triangle with a 3-inch (7.5 cm) base, with the edges aligned along the diagonal centerline. Smooth flat.

7 Fold the upper left edge under to meet the diagonal centerline, forming a narrower triangle on the upper left side.

8 Fold the lower right edge under to meet the diagonal centerline, forming a narrower triangle on the lower right side.

9 Rotate the napkin so the point is facing up. Tuck the upper half of the napkin under, forming a flat upper edge.

10 Arrange the napkin with the flat edge facing down.

#63 Heart

This sweet fold is perfect for Valentine's Day, but it's also welcome anytime you're making a meal for those you love. The Heart fold works well in medium- to heavyweight fabrics with small to medium prints — like the bright pink with white polka dots I used here. It's pretty in solid colors, too. Iron the napkins with spray starch before you begin, and gently press them again after folding to help the heart hold its shape. A delicious cookie place card, a handwritten card or a small wrapped present would be great toppers for this fold.

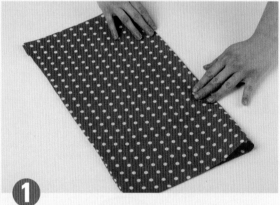

1 Lay the napkin out as a diamond, with the finished side facing down and the seamed edges facing up. Fold the lower left edge up to the upper right edge, forming a rectangle.

2 Fold the lower left edge up to the upper right edge again, forming a narrower rectangle.

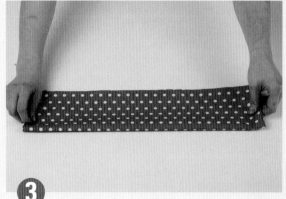

3 Rotate the napkin so that the fold is at the top and the loose edges are at the bottom.

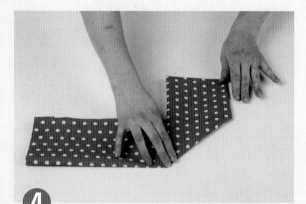

4 Holding the middle of the upper edge with your left hand, use your right hand to fold the right half of the upper edge down to the vertical centerline of the napkin.

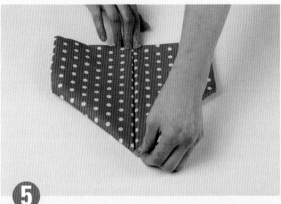

5 Fold the left half of the upper edge down to the vertical centerline of the napkin.

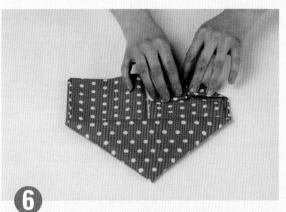

6 Flip the napkin over, keeping the point up and the tails down. Working on the left tail, fold the lower right and left corners in to meet at the vertical centerline of the tail, forming a point.

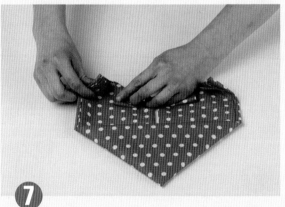

7 Working on the right tail, fold the lower right and left corners in to meet at the vertical centerline of the tail, forming a point.

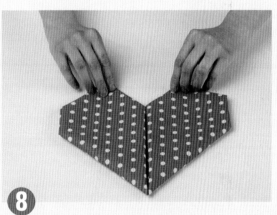

8 Flip the napkin over and arrange a heart at each place with the point facing down.

#⁶⁴Herb Pot

This pretty fold works well with smaller napkins in a thicker fabric, such as the ivory and green herb pattern I chose. Iron napkins with spray starch for the best results; after folding, gently press. Tuck a few fresh herb sprigs inside each pot for a lovely scent that complements what you're serving. For a completely different look, use black or orange napkins and candy eyes to turn this herb pot into a Halloween cat.

1 Lay the napkin out as a square, with the finished side facing down and the seamed edges facing up.

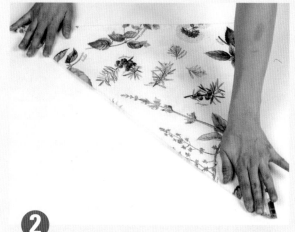

2 Fold the upper right corner down to the lower left corner, forming a triangle.

3 Rotate the napkin so that the longest side is at the top. Fold the lower point up to the center of the napkin.

4 Fold the upper edge down to the center to meet the point.

5 Holding the middle of the upper edge with your left hand, use your right hand to fold the right point over and down to the left, aligning the lower edges of the napkin and leaving a tail on the lower left side.

6 Fold the left point over and down to the right, aligning the lower edges of the napkin and leaving a tail on the lower right side.

7 Flip the napkin over and arrange with the flat edge facing down and the points facing up.

#65 High Tower

This fold can be used as a pocket for utensils, set to the left of each plate, or it can be arranged atop each dinner plate. It works with any color or pattern, in any fabric weight; I chose a solid dark blue napkin. Iron napkins with spray starch before folding, and lightly press after folding.

1 Lay the napkin out as a square, with the finished side facing down and the seamed edges facing up.

2 Fold the upper left corner down toward the lower right corner, leaving about 2 inches (5 cm) of the bottom layer showing.

3 Flip the napkin over, arranging it with the longest side at the top.

4 Working with the upper left point, fold the top third of the left side down, aligning the edges on the left side.

5 Working with the upper right point, fold the top third of the right side down, aligning the edges on the right side.

6 Fold the upper edge down about 2 inches (5 cm).

7 Flip the napkin over, keeping the flat edge at the top.

8 Fold the left point one-third of the way over to the right point.

9 Fold the right point over so that the point touches the left edge. Arrange a napkin at each place with the point facing up.

#66 Little Bird

Recreate this pretty fold with any solid or patterned napkin that suits your theme; I chose a blue and white pattern that would be well suited to a brunch, lunch or casual cookout. Light- to medium-weight fabrics work best, as they won't get too thick with the multiple folds required for this design. Starch and press napkins before you begin folding.

1 Lay the napkin out as a square, with the finished side facing down and the seamed edges facing up.

2 Fold the lower right corner up to the upper left corner, forming a triangle.

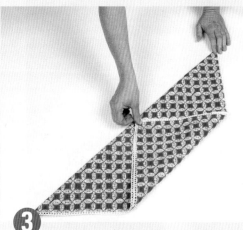

3 Fold the upper left corner down to the middle of the lower right edge.

4 Holding the middle of the lower right edge with your right hand, use your left hand to fold the lower left point up at an angle toward the right.

5 Fold the right tip over to the left, overlapping the previous fold and aligning all edges along the lower left, forming a point on the lower right side.

6 Using one-third of the napkin's height, fold the end with two points over toward the lower right point.

7 Fold the lower left point underneath the napkin to meet the upper right point, folding the napkin in half.

8 Fold the lower right point down to form the bird's head. Arrange a bird at each place.

#**67** Lotus

This is a beautiful fold to place between a plate and a bowl. It's also gorgeous arranged in a shallow bowl, where it looks a little like an artichoke. I chose a medium blue napkin, but you can use any color or pattern, in any fabric weight. Iron napkins with spray starch before folding.

1 Lay the napkin out as a square, with the finished side facing down and the seamed edges facing up.

2 Fold the lower left corner in to the center of the napkin.

3 Fold the lower right corner in to the center.

4 Fold the top left and top right corners in to the center, forming a diamond.

5 Fold the bottom point up to the center.

6 Fold the top point down to the center.

7 Fold the left point and right point in to the center, forming a square.

8 Flip the napkin over, keeping it arranged as a square. Fold the lower left and lower right corners in to the center.

10 Holding the center of the diamond steady with your left hand, use your right hand to reach underneath the right point and find the center point beneath it. Gently pull that point out to form a petal.

9 Fold the upper left and upper right corners in to the center, forming a diamond.

11 Holding the center of the diamond steady with your right hand, use your left hand to reach underneath the top point and find the center point beneath it. Gently pull that point out to form a petal.

12 Repeat on the bottom and left points. Holding the center of the diamond steady with your right hand, use your left hand to reach underneath each point and find the center point beneath it. Gently pull each center point out to form a petal.

13 Adjust petals as necessary and arrange a lotus at each place.

#**68** Orchid 1

This soft, elegant fold is arranged in a wineglass; alternatively, you could pull the end of the fold through a napkin ring and lay it flat on a dinner plate. Use any fabric weight in any color or pattern you like, tailoring your choice to fit the occasion. I used a yellow patterned napkin. Iron napkins with spray starch before folding, and have one wineglass, water glass or napkin ring per napkin ready before you begin folding.

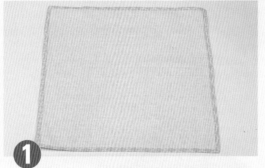

1 Lay the napkin out as a square, with the finished side facing down and the seamed edges facing up.

2 Fold the lower edge up to the upper edge, forming a horizontal rectangle.

3 Fold the upper right point down to the middle of the lower edge.

4 Fold the upper left point down to the middle of the lower edge, forming a triangle.

5 Fold the lower right point up to meet the upper point.

6 Fold the lower left point up to meet the upper point, forming a diamond.

7 Working with the right side of the diamond, lift the top layer of the upper point, put your thumbs inside the layers to open them up and fold the top 1 inch (2.5 cm) of the point to the right, forming a petal shape.

8 Working with the left side of the diamond, lift the top layer of the upper point, put your thumbs inside the layers to open them up and fold the top 1 inch (2.5 cm) of the point to the left, forming a petal shape.

9 Pick up the napkin from the bottom third, pinching about 1 inch (2.5 cm) of the bottom edge on each side to meet behind the napkin, with the right and left points still splayed to the sides.

10 Drop the napkin into a wineglass and gently arrange the petals.

#**69** Paper Football

Do you remember those paper footballs that bored school kids like to fold — and then throw at each other? This whimsical fold is a grownup version of that, rendered in cloth. It works in any color or pattern in a medium-weight fabric; I chose a striking chartreuse color here. Press napkins before folding.

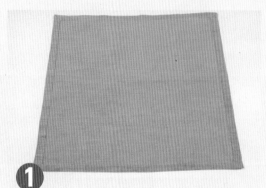

1 Lay the napkin out as a square, with the finished side facing down and the seamed edges facing up.

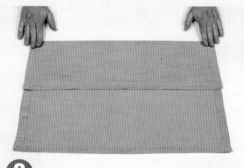

2 Fold the lower edge up toward the upper edge, using one-third the height of the napkin.

3 Fold the upper edge down to the lower edge, forming a horizontal rectangle.

4 Fold the upper right corner down toward the left, forming a point at the lower right corner.

5 Fold the angled right edge up to the upper edge, forming a triangle on top of the napkin.

6 Fold the angled right edge down to the lower edge, forming another triangle.

7 Fold the lower left corner up toward the right, forming a point at the upper left corner.

8 Tuck the upper left point under the top layer of triangle to secure it. Arrange a napkin at each place or on a buffet.

#**70** Parrot

Brightly striped fabrics really show off the shape of this napkin fold, but it will work with nearly any color or pattern. I used an aqua, orange, brown and gold striped napkin that gives the fold the tropical look I was after. This fold works best with medium- to heavyweight fabric; iron napkins with spray starch before folding. After folding, gently press the tail for a tailored look or leave it as is for a more casual look.

1 Lay the napkin out as a square, with the finished side facing down and the seamed edges facing up.

2 Fold the lower edge up to the upper edge, forming a horizontal rectangle.

3 Lift the top layer of the upper right corner with your left hand and use your right hand to fold the lower right corner inside the napkin to the vertical centerline.

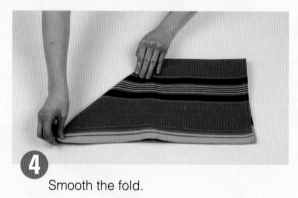

4 Smooth the fold.

5 Lift the top layer of the upper left corner with your right hand and use your left hand to fold the lower left corner inside the napkin to the vertical centerline.

6 Smooth out the large triangle.

7 Fold the left point of the triangle over to the right point, forming a smaller triangle.

8 Holding the triangle's lowest point with your right hand, use your left hand to fan out the four upper right points.

9 Flip the napkin over so that the points are at the upper left and the folded edge is at the lower right. Working from the folded edge, roll the napkin up about halfway.

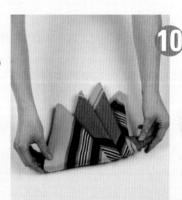

10 Flip the napkin over again and arrange the parrot.

#71 Peacock

Easier than it looks, this fold begins with a simple accordion-style pleat placed in a stemmed glass. The result is an exotic peacock design, with a tail that drapes dramatically down to the table. Heavyweight fabrics ironed with spray starch work best; I chose a dark blue brocade. You can use any color or pattern, but avoid large prints, as they will distract from the visual impact of the finished fold. Have one stemmed wineglass ready for each napkin.

1 Lay the napkin out as a square, with the finished side facing down and the seamed edges facing up.

2 Fold the lower right corner in about 2 inches (5 cm).

3 Fold the same edge under about 2 inches (5 cm).

4 Fold the same edge back over and under, accordion-style, aligning the edges.

5 Continue folding the napkin accordion-style.

6 When the napkin is completely folded to the upper left corner, pick it up and bend it about one-third from one end, placing the bend in a wineglass.

7 Arrange the short end as the peacock's head and fan out the long end, allowing it to drape down to the table as the peacock's tail.

#72 Pinwheel

This festive napkin fold enlivens the table for any casual occasion, whether for kids or adults. Solid or patterned napkins of any weight will work well; I chose a blue and white fruit pattern. Iron napkins with spray starch before folding, and gently press after folding.

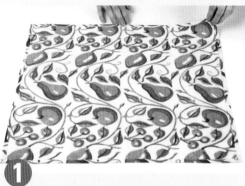

1 Lay the napkin out as a square, with the finished side facing down and the seamed edges facing up.

2 Fold the lower left corner in to the center of the napkin.

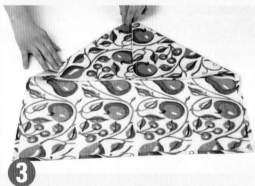

3 Fold the lower right corner in to the center.

4 Fold the upper left and upper right corners in to the center, forming a diamond.

5 Rotate the napkin and arrange it as a square. Fold the left edge over to the vertical centerline.

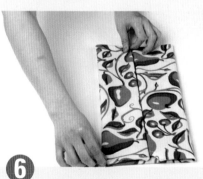

6 Fold the right edge over to the vertical centerline, forming a vertical rectangle.

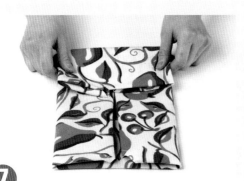

7 Fold the lower edge up to the horizontal centerline.

8 Fold the upper edge down to the horizontal centerline, forming a square.

9 Loosen the two tips from inside the top layer at the left side of the square, gently pulling them out to form a point.

10 Loosen the two tips from inside the top layer at the right side of the square, gently pulling them out to form a point.

11 Fold the upper half of the left point so that it points straight up, perpendicular to its original position.

12 Fold the lower half of the right point so that it points straight down, perpendicular to its original position.

#73 Pointed Pocket

Slip your silverware into this pretty pocket for a beautiful presentation. While this fold works well with any color, solids show off its multiple layers better than patterns; I chose a solid bright yellow napkin. Keep in mind, too, that a portion of the napkin's reverse side will be visible in the finished fold. For very finished-looking results, press the fabric both before and after folding.

1 Lay the napkin out as a diamond, with the finished side facing down and the seamed edges facing up. Fold the lower left edge up to the upper right edge, forming a rectangle.

2 Fold the lower right edge up to the upper left edge, forming a diamond.

3 Fold the top layer of the upper point down toward the lower point, leaving 1/2 inch (1 cm) of the bottom layer showing.

4 Fold the next layer of the upper point down toward the lower point, leaving 1/2 inch (1 cm) of the previous layer showing.

5 Fold the third layer of the upper point down toward the lower point, leaving ½ inch (1 cm) of the previous layer showing.

6 Flip the napkin over, keeping the same point at the bottom. Fold the left point over toward the right, using one-third the width of the napkin.

7 Fold the right point over to the left edge, overlapping the previous fold.

8 Flip the napkin over and arrange it with the long point down.

#74 Pouf

This soft, festive napkin design is anchored in a wineglass, with a collection of little poufs at the top and no visible folds. You can dress it up by using a silky napkin or make it more causal with a fun print, such as the multicolored floral napkin I used here. This fold works best with unstarched pressed napkins in a lightweight fabric. The smaller the glass you plan to use, the lighter the fabric should be.

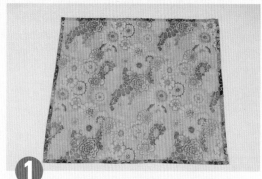

1 Lay the napkin out as a square, with the finished side facing down and the seamed edges facing up.

2 Fold the lower edge up to the upper edge, forming a horizontal rectangle.

3 Fold the right edge over to the left edge, forming a square.

4 Rotate the napkin and arrange it as a diamond, with the loose edges at the top.

5 Fold the lower point up halfway to the center of the napkin.

6 Fold the right point over to meet the left point.

7 Fold the top layer back over to the right, using about two-thirds the width of the lower edge.

8 Fold the right point back over to the left, aligning the right edge with the layer beneath.

9 Fold the tip of the top layer back over to the right, touching the tip to the right edge.

10 Flip the napkin over, keeping the point up. Fold the right tip over to the left, aligning the right edge with the layers beneath.

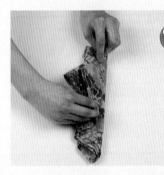

11 Fold the left tip back over to the right, aligning the left edge with the layers beneath.

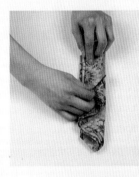

12 Fold the tip of the top layer back over to the left, touching the tip to the left edge.

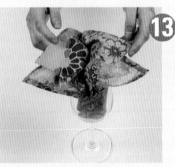

13 Drop the napkin into a wineglass, with the points up, and gently separate the four top points, bending the middle two away from each other.

14 Tuck the two right points in toward each other and the two left points in toward each other, puffing each one up as you tuck, to form four small poufs.

#75 Reveal

This fold is designed to show off a double-sided napkin. The finished design is a simple diamond with a small portion peeled back to reveal the napkin's reverse side. I chose a pretty red, green and yellow napkin with a floral design on one side and stripes on the other. Any fabric weight works. Iron napkins with spray starch before folding. After folding, gently press for a tailored look or leave as is for a more casual look.

1 Lay the napkin out as a square, with the finished side facing down and the seamed edges facing up.

2 Fold the lower edge up to the upper edge, forming a horizontal rectangle.

3 Fold the left edge up to the upper edge.

4 Fold the right edge up to the upper edge, forming a triangle.

5 Flip the napkin over, keeping the same point down.

6 Fold the left point down to the lower point.

7 Fold the right point down to the lower point, forming a diamond.

8 Working with the top layer, pick up the lower left tip and peel back the outermost layer 1 to 2 inches (2.5 to 5 cm) to the left to reveal the fabric on the reverse side. Smooth to flatten.

9 Working with the top layer, pick up the lower right tip and peel back the outermost layer 1 to 2 inches (2.5 to 5 cm) to the right to reveal the fabric on the reverse side. Smooth to flatten. Arrange the napkin with the revealed points up.

#76 Shawl

This napkin fold looks like a shawl wrapped around the shoulders and overlapping in front, making it perfect for a ladies' gathering. If possible, use a double-sided napkin, since both sides will show. I chose a napkin with a yellow and green floral pattern on one side and coordinating stripes on the other. Any fabric weight works with this fold. Iron with spray starch before folding. After folding, gently press for a tailored look or leave as is for a more casual look.

1 Lay the napkin out as a square, with the finished side facing down and the seamed edges facing up.

2 Fold the upper left corner in to the center of the napkin.

3 Fold the newly folded edge over again, taking it just past the center point of the napkin.

4 Flip the napkin over, arranging it with the flat fold at the top. Fold the lower point up to the original center of the napkin.

5 Fold the newly folded lower edge up, taking it just past the point in the center.

6 Fold the left point down and to the right, so that the tail hangs past the lower edge of the napkin with its lower edge parallel to the napkin.

7 Fold the right point down and to the left, placing the right tail on top of the left tail and aligning the lower edges.

#77 Stairway

With a finished fold that stands upright on the plate, mimicking the ascent of a spiral staircase, this is a dramatically stylish presentation. While any color or pattern will do, be sure to choose a thick, sturdy fabric, such as the brown woven napkin with a subtle border that I used here, and iron napkins with plenty of spray starch before folding. For the crispest results, press the napkin again before rolling it and standing it upright.

1 Lay the napkin out as a square, with the finished side facing down and the seamed edges facing up.

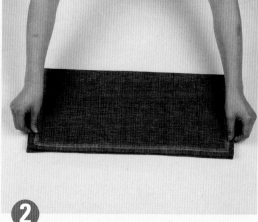

2 Fold the lower edge up to the upper edge, forming a horizontal rectangle.

3 Lift the top layer of the upper right corner with your left hand and use your right hand to fold the lower right corner inside the napkin to the vertical centerline.

4 Lift the top layer of the upper left corner with your right hand and use your left hand to fold the lower left corner inside the napkin to the vertical centerline, forming a triangle.

5 Fold the left side of the triangle over to the right side, forming a smaller triangle. Press all four layers of the points, if desired.

6 Starting at the left side of the triangle, roll up the napkin, keeping it aligned at the upper edge.

7 Continue rolling the napkin almost to the end. Stand the napkin up on the wider end, holding it upright.

8 Fan out the four points at the base of the napkin, allowing it to stand upright and creating a spiral staircase effect.

#**78** Straight to the Point

This napkin fold can be arranged flat or standing upright at each place. If you choose the latter presentation, consider tucking a candy, small favor or dinner roll into the center of each. This fold works well with medium- to heavyweight fabrics in any solid or patterned fabric. I chose a colorful floral print with bright teals and pinks on a chartreuse background. If you plan to stand the finished napkins up, it's important to starch the fabric. Either way, iron them before folding.

1 Lay the napkin out as a square, with the finished side facing down and the seamed edges facing up.

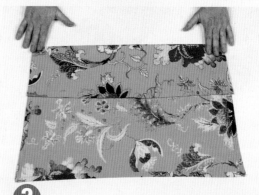

2 Fold the lower edge up toward the upper edge, using one-third the height of the napkin.

3 Fold the upper edge down to the lower edge, forming a horizontal rectangle.

4 Holding the middle of the upper edge with your left hand, use your right hand to fold the right half of the upper edge down to the vertical centerline of the napkin.

5 Fold the left half of the upper edge down to the vertical centerline, forming a triangle with two tails hanging below it.

6 Fold the lower edge of the right tail up to meet the base of the triangle.

7 Fold the right tail up again, forming a band along the bottom of the right side of the triangle.

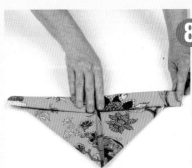

8 Fold the lower edge of the right tail up to meet the base of the triangle. Fold the left tail up again, forming a band along the bottom of the left side of the triangle.

9 Fold the right side over toward the left, using one-third the width of the napkin.

10 Fold the left side over to the right, tucking it behind the top layer to secure it. Arrange a napkin point side up at each place. Alternatively, open up the base and stand the napkin upright.

#79 A Tisket, a Tasket

This cheerful fold incorporates two napkins; it works best with light- to medium-weight napkins, one a solid color and one patterned. I paired a solid dark pink napkin with a yellow print. Iron napkins with spray starch before folding; after folding, gently press for a tailored look or leave as is for a more casual look. As a finishing touch, tuck a place card, a small party favor or a sprig of herbs into each basket.

1 Lay the solid-color napkin out as a square, with the finished side facing down and the seamed edges facing up. Place the patterned napkin on top as an offset square, with the finished side facing down and the seamed edges facing up, leaving about 1 inch (2.5 cm) of the solid-color napkin showing at the left and upper edges.

2 Fold the lower right corner of the patterned napkin up to the upper left corner of the patterned napkin, forming a triangle atop a square.

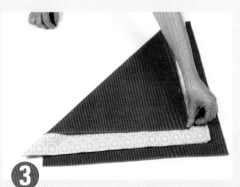

3 Fold the lower right corner of the solid-color napkin up toward the upper left corner of both napkins, forming a triangle with three staggered layers showing.

4 Flip the napkins over and arrange with the folded flat edge at the bottom.

5 Holding the middle of the lower edge with your left hand, use your right hand to fold the right point up toward the upper point, forming a vertical centerline.

6 Fold the left point up toward the upper point, forming a diamond.

7 Flip the napkin over, keeping the same point up. Holding the lower point with your left hand, use your right hand to fold the right point over to the vertical centerline.

8 Holding the lower point with your right hand, use your left hand to fold the left point over to the vertical centerline.

9 Using a little less than half the napkin's height, fold the lower point under, creating a flat lower edge.

10 Arrange the napkin with the flat edge down.

#80 Triple Layer

This design gets its name from the three layers that show in the finished fold. To make the most of the presentation, choose a double-sided napkin, such as the green floral with solid red reverse side I used here. Iron napkins with spray starch before folding. After folding, gently press for a tailored look or leave as is for a more casual look.

1 Lay the napkin out as a square, with the finished side facing down and the seamed edges facing up.

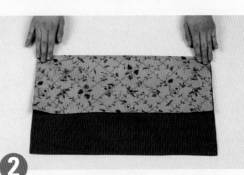

2 Fold the lower edge up toward the upper edge, using one-third the height of the napkin.

3 Working with the top layer, fold the upper edge halfway down to the lower edge of the napkin.

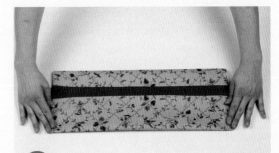

4 Fold the upper edge down enough to just cover the upper fold, forming a horizontal rectangle with three bands.

5 Flip the napkin over, keeping the same edges up and down. Fold the right edge over toward the left, creating a vertical band about 2 inches (5 cm) wide.

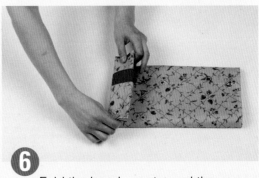

6 Fold the band over toward the left again.

7 Fold the band over toward the left a third time.

8 Fold the left edge over toward the right, creating a vertical band about 2 inches (5 cm) wide.

9 Fold the band over toward the right two more times, until the left side either overlaps the right side (as in the photo at left) or meets the right side (as in the photo below).

#81 Tuxedo

This fold offers each guest two napkins, the black for dinner and the white for dessert (or vice versa). The two-tone color scheme features both napkins in crisp diagonal stripes. While the black and white combination is formal, this design is very flexible, working well with any two colors — or a solid color with a coordinated patterned napkin. Iron all napkins with spray starch before folding; after folding, gently press.

1 Lay the first napkin out as a square, with the finished side facing down and the seamed edges facing up. Lay the second napkin out as a square on top of the first napkin, with the finished side facing down and the seamed edges facing up.

2 Holding both lower edges together, fold the lower edges up to the upper edges, forming a horizontal rectangle.

3 Fold the right edge over to the left edge, forming a square.

4 Working with the top layer only, fold the upper left corner back about 1 inch (2.5 cm).

5 Fold that corner down again, repeating the fold about three more times until the top napkin forms a band that divides the square diagonally.

6 Working with the top layer of the upper left corner, tuck the corner under itself just far enough to leave a 1-inch (2.5 cm) band of napkin showing parallel to the first band.

7 Working with the next three layers of the upper left corner, fold the corners over and tuck them under the previous band far enough to leave another 1-inch (2.5 cm) band of napkin showing parallel to the first and second bands.

8 Flip the napkin over, keeping the same edges up and down. Fold the right edge over toward the left edge, forming a 2-inch (5 cm) wide vertical band.

9 Fold the left edge almost to the right edge, overlapping the previous fold.

10 Flip the napkin over.

#82 Two-Headed Fish

To me, this design looks a little like a two-headed fish — thus the name — but given that it's a pretty abstract representation, you can use it for nearly any occasion. It works best with a medium- to heavyweight fabric, in any color or pattern; I used a bright yellow and white fruit pattern. Iron napkins with spray starch before folding, and gently press them after folding.

1 Lay the napkin out as a square, with the finished side facing down and the seamed edges facing up.

2 Fold the lower left corner in to the center of the napkin.

3 Fold the lower right corner in to the center.

4 Fold the upper right and upper left corners in to the center, forming a diamond.

5 Holding the napkin by the middle of the upper left and lower right sides, carefully pick it up and tuck the upper right side under the lower left side.

6 Arrange the napkin as a horizontal rectangle, with the middle triangle pointing up.

7 Fold the left edge over to the right edge, forming a square.

8 Fold the top layer of the lower right corner up to the upper left corner.

9 Fold the top layer of the upper left corner under itself twice to form a narrow band.

10 Fold the top layer of the lower right corner under itself twice to form a narrow band.

11 Flip the napkin over, arranging it as a diamond with a vertical crease. Fold the left and right points in to meet at the center.

12 Flip the napkin back over and arrange it on a plate.

#**83** Viking

This napkin fold gets its name from its resemblance to a horned Viking helmet. I played up the connection by using a fabric with a Nordic-style pattern, in natural shades of rust, brown and cream. Choose medium-weight napkins in any color or pattern, and starch the napkins before ironing them if you plan to stand the finished folds upright.

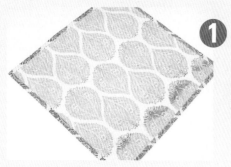

1 Lay the napkin out as a diamond, with the finished side facing down and the seamed edges facing up.

2 Fold the upper point down to the lower point, forming a triangle.

3 Fold the right point down to the lower point.

4 Fold the left point down to the lower point, forming a diamond.

5 Fold the top layer of the lower left tip up to the upper tip, forming a small triangle on the upper left half of the diamond.

6 Fold the top layer of the lower right tip up to the upper tip, forming a small triangle on the upper right half of the diamond.

7 Working with the small triangle at the upper left, fold the upper tip down toward the left, forming a small triangle with a tip that hangs past the upper left edge of the diamond.

8 Working with the small triangle at the upper right, fold the upper tip down toward the right, forming a small triangle with a tip that hangs past the upper right edge of the diamond.

9 Fold the lower point of the diamond up toward the upper point, leaving about 2 inches (5 cm) of the bottom layer showing.

10 Flip the napkin over, keeping the same point at the top.

11 Fold the lower edge about 1 inch (2.5 cm) underneath the napkin, forming a band.

12 Fold the right tip over toward the left, using about one-third the width of the napkin.

13 Fold the left tip over toward the right, tucking it under the top layer of the previous fold to secure it.

14 Flip the napkin over and arrange it with the flat edge down. Alternatively, open up the base and stand the napkin upright.

#84 Wave

Use this fold as a pretty pocket for utensils or a place card; you can place each utensil behind a different wave, if you like. I used a medium blue napkin here to play up the watery look, but it works well with any color or pattern in any fabric weight. Iron napkins with spray starch before folding, and lightly press after folding.

1 Lay the napkin out as a square, with the finished side facing down and the seamed edges facing up.

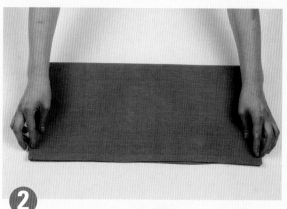

2 Fold the lower edge up to the upper edge, forming a horizontal rectangle.

3 Lift the top layer of the upper right corner with your left hand and use your right hand to fold the lower right corner inside the napkin to the vertical centerline.

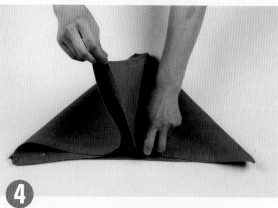

4 Lift the top layer of the upper left corner with your right hand and use your left hand to fold the lower left corner inside the napkin to the vertical centerline, forming a triangle.

5 Fold the left point of the triangle over to the right point, forming a smaller triangle.

6 Holding the bottom point steady with your right hand, use your left hand to fan out four layers of points at the upper right side.

7 Tuck the bottom point under to meet the upper left corner, aligning the left edges.

8 Arrange the napkin vertically. For placing napkin over utensils as in the picture below, simply twist end under.

#85 Whale's Tail

For each finished fold, you'll need to have one water glass or wineglass ready.
A solid white napkin would dress this design up for a more formal party.
A bright multicolored stripe, such as the yellow, green, tan and red napkin
I used here, makes this a fun fold for a party with a Mexican theme. Use
lightly starched and pressed medium-weight cloth napkins.

1 Lay the napkin out as a square, with the finished side facing down and the seamed edges facing up.

2 Fold the upper edge down to the lower edge, forming a horizontal rectangle.

3 Fold the right edge over to the left edge, forming a square.

4 Fold the upper right corner in toward the center, using about 1½ inches (4 cm) of fabric to form a small triangle.

5 Fold triangle under napkin and then over napkin again, accordion-style.

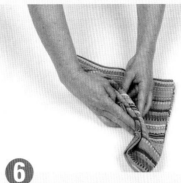

6 Make two more accordion folds in the napkin, leaving the lower left corner of the napkin unfolded.

7 Turn the napkin so that the accordion folds are at the lower edge and pick up the napkin by the accordion folds, folding it in half.

8 Drop the napkin into a glass.

#86 Wide Collar

This versatile fold works well with solid-color or patterned napkins, and can go formal or casual. I chose a solid-color napkin with a decorative border, which shows up nicely in the finished fold. Light- to medium-weight napkins work best. Begin this fold with pressed starched napkins and press the finished fold again, if necessary, to keep the two sides of the collar lying flat. Tuck a flower, place card or small favor inside each finished napkin, if you like.

1 Lay the napkin out as a square, with the finished side facing down and the seamed edges facing up.

2 Fold the lower right corner up to the upper left corner, forming a triangle.

3 Fold the lower left point up to the upper left corner, aligning the left edges.

4 Fold the upper right point over to the upper left corner, forming a square.

5 Flip the napkin over, arranging it with the loose edges at the lower right corner.

6 Fold the lower right corner up to the upper left corner, forming a triangle.

7 Fold the lower left point over toward the upper right point, using about one-third the length of the diagonal and aligning the edges at the lower right.

8 Fold the upper right point down toward the lower left edge, tucking it underneath the top layer of the previous fold.

9 Arrange the napkin with the point facing down. Working with the top layer of the point, fold the left half out to the left and the right half out to the right. Press the points to keep them flat, if necessary.

10 Arrange the napkin with the point facing up.

#87 Wings

This pretty upright napkin fold looks ready for takeoff, with a wing balancing it on either side. You can make a small version using luncheon napkins or a larger version using dinner napkins. Use fabric in any weight and in any color or pattern; I chose a dark gold fringed napkin. Iron napkins with spray starch before folding.

1 Lay the napkin out as a diamond, with the finished side facing down and the seamed edges facing up.

2 Fold the bottom point up to the top point, forming a triangle.

3 Fold the left point up to the upper point.

4 Fold the right point up to the upper point, forming a diamond.

5 Fold the lower point up toward the upper point, leaving about 1 inch (2.5 cm) of the bottom layer showing.

6 Working with the top layer, fold the upper point down to the lower edge.

7 Flip the napkin over, arranging it with the flat fold at the bottom.

8 Fold the left point over to the right, using about one-third the width of the napkin and aligning the lower edges.

9 Fold the right point over to the left, tucking it into the pocket at the left.

10 Stand the napkin fold up, gently squeezing the sides together to form a circular base. Fold the left point down.

11 Fold the right point down.

Advanced Napkin Folds

#88 Aloha Shirt

To play up the fun, casual look of this fold, choose a tropical-looking fabric, like the dark yellow and orange patterned napkin I used here. This fold works well with fabrics of any weight, color or pattern — select something that suits your occasion, from team colors to Hawaiian prints. Iron napkins with spray starch before folding, and gently press again after folding to help napkins keep their shape (this will be particularly necessary with smaller or thicker napkins).

1 Lay the napkin out as a square, with the finished side facing down and the seamed edges facing up.

2 Fold the left edge to the vertical centerline of the napkin.

3 Fold the right edge to the vertical centerline.

4 Fold the lower edge under about 1 inch (2.5 cm).

5 Fold the lower left corner in to touch the vertical centerline, creating a narrow triangle on the left that will represent half of the shirt's collar.

6 Fold the lower right corner in to touch the vertical centerline, creating a narrow triangle on the right that will represent the other half of the shirt's collar.

7 Holding the center of the napkin steady with your right hand, use your left hand to pick up the top layer at the upper left and fold the loose corner back, forming a narrow triangle on the left.

8 Holding the center of the napkin steady with your left hand, use your right hand to pick up the top layer at the upper right and fold the loose corner back, forming a narrow triangle on the right.

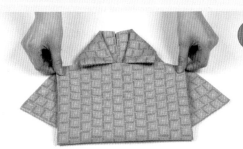

9 Fold the upper edge down to the collar, tucking the edge beneath both tips of the collar.

#89 Bamboo

This sweet little fold is suitable for smaller dishes, so perch it atop salad or dessert plates. Use a thicker napkin, as lightweight fabric won't give you the body you need. Any color or pattern will work; I chose a napkin with a yellow background and a light blue toile pattern. Press napkins with spray starch before folding.

1 Lay the napkin out as a square, with the finished side facing down and the seamed edges facing up.

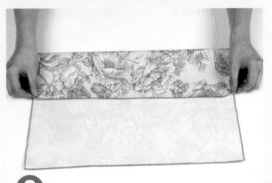

2 Fold the lower edge up toward the upper edge, using one-third the height of the napkin.

3 Fold the upper edge down to the lower edge, forming a horizontal rectangle.

4 Holding the middle of the lower edge with your right hand, use your left hand to fold the left half of the lower edge up to the vertical centerline of the napkin.

5 Fold the right half of the lower edge up to the vertical centerline, forming a triangle with two tails rising above it.

6 Fold the upper edge of the left tail down, aligning the top of the fold with the layer beneath it.

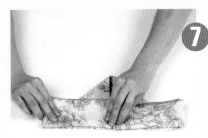

7 Fold the upper edge of the right tail down, aligning the top of the fold with the layer beneath it.

8 Rotate the napkin so that the point faces right. Fold the lower half up over the upper half.

9 Lift the top layer of the upper edge.

10 Tuck the upper edge of the top layer under into the fold.

11 Tuck the upper edge of the bottom layer over into the fold.

12 Stand the napkin up vertically on the flat base, holding the layers together.

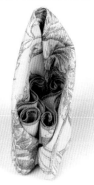

13 Arrange the napkin fold with the tall side at the back, exposing the inner layers.

#90 Bird of Paradise

This striking fold is well worth the effort. To mimic the bright hues of the tropical flower with this name, choose a napkin with at least some orange in it, like this wavy orange, brown, pink and gold striped pattern. With this many folds, softer fabrics work better than thick, stiff fabrics. Press but don't starch the napkins before folding. For the final presentation, you can place this napkin upright or flat on each plate; it looks great either way.

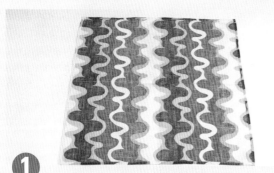

1 Lay the napkin out as a square, with the finished side facing down and the seamed edges facing up.

2 Fold the lower edge up to the upper edge, forming a horizontal rectangle.

3 Fold the left edge over to the right edge, forming a square.

4 Rotate the square to make a diamond, with the folded edge at the lower left and the loose points at the top. Fold the upper point down to the lower point, forming a triangle.

5 Holding the lower point with your right hand, use your left hand to fold the left point up to the vertical centerline of the napkin.

6 Holding the lower point with your left hand, use your right hand to fold the right point up to the vertical centerline, forming a kite shape.

7 Tuck the top of the kite under, forming a triangle.

8 Rotate the napkin 90 degrees to make an arrow pointing to the left. Bring the upper and lower points closer together underneath the napkin to prop it up.

9 Holding the upper and lower points loosely together with your right hand, use your left hand to gently pull up one layer at a time from the left point, using the four top layers to create a petal-like effect.

#91 Clamshell

The key to this design holding its shape is using a heavyweight fabric ironed well with lots of spray starch. I chose a solid dark blue napkin, but any color or pattern will work as long as the fabric is stiff enough. The effort is well worth it for the showy double fan that stands upright at each place. This fold makes a great first impression.

1 Lay the napkin out as a square, with the finished side facing down and the seamed edges facing up.

2 Fold the lower edge up to the horizontal centerline of the napkin.

3 Fold the upper edge down to the horizontal centerline.

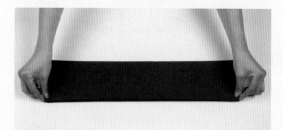

4 Fold the lower edge up to the upper edge, forming a thin horizontal rectangle.

5 Fold the left edge over to the right edge.

6 Holding the left edge in place with your left hand, use your right hand to fold the top layer of the right edge back over to the left, leaving about 1 inch (2.5 cm) of the left edge closed.

7 Fold the left edge back over toward the right edge, aligning the folds at the left.

8 Continue folding the top layer, accordion-style, until you reach the end.

9 Flip the napkin over, arranging it with the stack of folds on the right. Fold the left edge over to the right, aligning the folds at the left.

10 Continue folding the top layer, accordion-style, until you reach the end.

11 Stand the napkin up on one short edge, with the side exposing more layers up.

12 Fan out the edges of the napkin, pulling apart the two layers at each fold to make diamond-like designs visible from above the napkin.

13 Place the base of the napkin on the table and let it fan out to the sides.

#92 Dutch Baby

This cute little fold looks most elegant when done with a white napkin (as on the bottom of page 207), but it will work in any color or pattern. Here, I chose a solid blue fabric. Because of the many layers of folds, light- to medium-weight fabrics work best. Iron napkins with spray starch before folding.

1 Lay the napkin out as a square, with the finished side facing down and the seamed edges facing up.

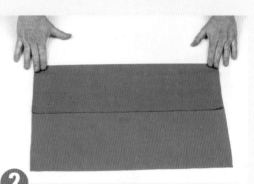

2 Fold the lower edge up toward the upper edge, using one-third the height of the napkin.

3 Fold the upper edge down to the lower edge, forming a horizontal rectangle.

4 Fold the right edge to the vertical centerline of the napkin.

5 Fold the left edge to the vertical centerline.

6 Fold the right half of the lower edge up to the vertical centerline.

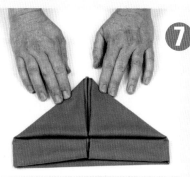

7 Fold the lower left edge up to the vertical centerline, forming a downward-pointing arrow.

8 Flip the napkin over, keeping the point down.

9 Fold the flat right edge of the arrow over to the left and down so that what was the upper right edge of the arrow now forms a horizontal line across the lower third of the napkin.

10 Fold the flat left edge of the arrow over to the right and down, overlapping the previous fold, so that what was the upper left edge of the arrow now forms a horizontal line across the lower third of the napkin. Tuck the corner under the top layer of the previous fold to secure it.

11 Flip the napkin over, arranging it with the wider end down. Open up the inside of the napkin into a rounded base.

12 Stand the napkin upright on its base.

#93 Elf Boot

This fanciful design is perfect for a Christmastime table when made with a red or green napkin; otherwise, any color or pattern will work well. Use a medium-weight fabric — you want some heft for stability but not so much that the napkin gets too thick with multiple folds — and lightly starch and press napkins before folding. Arrange a finished boot atop each plate, with a Christmas ornament, perhaps. The Elf Boot fold could also be used as a fairy slipper for a party with a Midsummer Night's Dream *theme.*

1 Lay the napkin out as a square, with the finished side facing down and the seamed edges facing up.

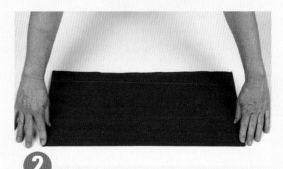

2 Fold the upper edge down to the lower edge.

3 Fold the upper edge down to the lower edge again, forming a narrow horizontal rectangle.

4 Holding the middle of the upper edge with your left hand, use your right hand to fold the right half of the upper edge down to the vertical centerline.

5 Fold the left half of the upper edge down to the vertical centerline.

6 Fold the upper right edge down to the vertical centerline.

7 Fold the upper left edge down to the vertical centerline.

8 Fold the left half of the napkin over the right half.

9 Flip the napkin over, keeping the same point at the top.

10 Fold the top layer of the lower edge over to the right, perpendicular to the napkin.

11 Fold the lower right corner up to the left edge, forming a small triangle.

12 Fold the lower point up, tucking it underneath the upper triangle to secure it.

13 The result will be a boot shape.

14 Stand the boot up on its base, with the toe pointing away from you.

15 Insert your thumbs inside the upper layers and fold them down over the boot. Arrange a finished boot at each place.

#94 Hummingbird

This challenging yet fun fold can be made with nearly any type of napkin: fabric weight doesn't matter, nor does the pattern. I chose a solid deep green napkin here; another example of the Hummingbird fold appears at the bottom of page 211, where I used a silky gray organza fabric. Iron napkins with spray starch before folding, then press again after folding to help them hold the shape.

1 Lay the napkin out as a diamond, with the finished side facing down and the seamed edges facing up.

2 Fold the right point in toward the lower middle of the napkin until the left edge creates a vertical centerline.

3 Fold the left point in toward the lower middle of the napkin until the right edge meets the vertical centerline, forming a kite shape.

4 Fold the bottom point up, forming a large triangle with a smaller triangle at the base.

5 Fold the lower edge up far enough to just cover the top point of the smaller triangle.

6 Fold the right edge over to the left edge.

7 Fold the top layer of the lower left corner up in a small triangle, aligning the upper left edges.

8 Flip the napkin over. Fold the lower right corner up in a small triangle, aligning the upper edges, forming the tail. Press gently.

9 Working with the longest point, fold it under about halfway up the napkin, extending the tip out in the opposite direction from the tail.

10 Using the top third of the same point, gently lift the point and open it slightly to work with a flat triangle.

11 Fold the point down inside the fold about 2 inches (5 cm), then back up, extending it out about 1 inch (2.5 cm). Fold the point closed, forming the hummingbird's head.

12 Flip the napkin over and spread the tail points apart slightly.

#95 Luna Moth

Use this design for a garden party — or anytime you want a fold that looks like it fluttered in for the occasion. It works well with any color or pattern, but be sure to use a medium-weight fabric ironed with lots of spray starch so that it holds its shape. I chose a gold and brown floral napkin, which makes the fold look like a butterfly. Press the ends of the wings after folding.

1 Lay the napkin out as a square, with the finished side facing down and the seamed edges facing up.

2 Fold the lower edge up to the upper edge, forming a horizontal rectangle.

3 Fold the right edge up to the upper edge.

4 Fold the left edge up to the upper edge, forming a triangle.

5 Flip the napkin over, keeping the same point down. Holding the lower point with your left hand, use your right hand to fold the lower right edge over to the vertical centerline, with the point extending above the napkin at the upper right.

6 Holding the lower point with your right hand, use your left hand to fold the lower left edge over to the vertical centerline, with the point extending above the napkin at the upper left, forming a kite shape.

7 Reach under the right half of the kite and pull the upper right corner from the middle of the kite out to the right.

8 Reach under the left half and pull the upper left corner from the middle out to the left, forming a diamond.

9 Flip the napkin over, keeping the same points up and down.

10 Fold the lower point up to the center of the diamond, then fold the lower edge up again, forming a triangle.

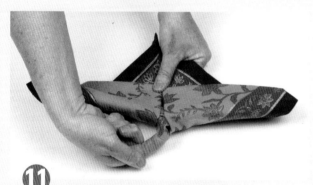

11 Reaching into the center of the base between the left and right sides, pull out the band slightly to separate the wings.

12 Separate the top points slightly and push the left and right sides together at the lower edge to elevate the center, forming a moth.

#96 Orchid 2

Use a water glass or wineglass to hold this flower-inspired napkin fold. While any fabric weight in any color or pattern will work, white fabric or silky solids lend an elegant look; I chose a deep maroon hue. This fold has softer, less visible lines than the Orchid 1 design (page 156), making it more flowing. Iron napkins with a little spray starch before folding. Have one glass ready for each napkin.

1 Lay the napkin out as a diamond, with the finished side facing down and the seamed edges facing up.

2 Fold the lower point up to the upper point, forming a triangle.

3 Fold the right point up to the upper point.

4 Fold the left point up to the upper point, forming a diamond.

5 Fold the lower right edge underneath the diamond to the vertical centerline.

6 Fold the lower left edge underneath the diamond to the vertical centerline.

7 Fold the lower point up to just below the upper point.

8 Bend the left and right sides back enough to fit the bottom of the napkin fold into a glass.

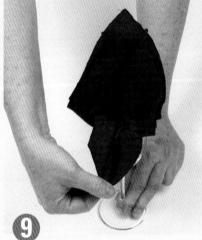

9 Bend the front layer forward to create a petal.

10 Bend the two points behind the front layer to either side, arranging them and the remaining top point into petals.

#**97** Rabbit

This cute rabbit will look like it hopped onto your table just for the party. Children and adults alike will appreciate its fun form, and will be reluctant to unfold it for its intended use. I used a cheerful cherry print, but it would be precious in any solid pastel color for a springtime party. This fold works best with a large thin napkin, such as a bandana, as the many folds stack up quickly.

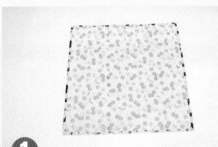

1 Lay the napkin out as a square, with the finished side facing down and the seamed edges facing up.

2 Fold the upper edge down to the lower edge.

3 Fold the upper edge down to the lower edge again, forming a narrow horizontal rectangle.

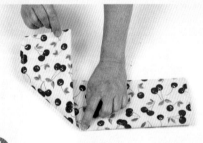

4 Holding the middle of the upper edge with your left hand, use your right hand to fold the right half of the upper edge down to the vertical centerline.

5 Fold the left half of the upper edge down to the vertical centerline.

6 Fold the lower right corner up to the center of the napkin.

7 Fold the lower left corner up to the center of the napkin, forming a diamond.

8 Fold the lower right edge to the vertical centerline.

9 Fold the lower left edge to the vertical centerline, forming a kite shape.

10 Flip the napkin over, keeping the same point up. Fold the upper point down, forming a triangle.

11 Flip the napkin over again, keeping the same flat edge at the top.

12 Fold the right point over toward the left, using about one-third the width of the napkin.

13 Fold the left point over toward the right, tucking it underneath the top layer of the previous fold.

14 Turn the napkin over and open up the folds of the two top points, forming ears.

15 Arrange a rabbit standing upright at each place.

#98 Swan

This fold works best with a thin fabric, but it needs to be stiff, too, so use plenty of starch and iron napkins before you begin folding. Choose a solid color so the layers of folds won't be obscured by a busy pattern. I used a light green napkin here, but white would be pretty, too. A classic fancy fold the likes of which you'd see on a cruise ship or in an old-school restaurant, the Swan design is great to pull out when you really want to impress. It's fun for a girls' night in, because ladies always appreciate such details.

1 Lay the napkin out as a square, with the finished side facing down and the seamed edges facing up.

2 Fold the upper edge down to the lower edge.

3 Fold the right edge over to the left edge, forming a square.

4 Arrange the square as a diamond, with the loose edges at the top. Holding the lower point with your left hand, use your right hand to fold the lower right edge over to the vertical centerline.

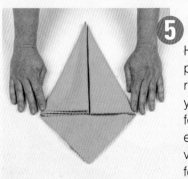

5 Holding the lower point with your right hand, use your left hand to fold the lower left edge over to the vertical centerline, forming a kite shape.

6 Flip the napkin over, keeping the same point up. Holding the lower point with your left hand, use your right hand to fold the lower right edge over to the vertical centerline.

7 Holding the lower point with your right hand, use your left hand to fold the lower left edge over to the vertical centerline.

8 Fold the lower point up to the upper point.

9 Fold the left and right sides of the napkin together underneath the napkin.

10 Stand the fold upright on its base.

11 Fold the narrower point over, forming the swan's head.

12 Working with the wider point, one layer at a time, separate the four layers, forming the swan's tail feathers.

13 Arrange a swan at each place, supported by its tail feathers.

#99 Tropics

You'll need two napkins for this fold, preferably contrasting ones. Try a solid-color napkin and a patterned one for a striking presentation. To play up the tropical look I wanted, I chose a solid magenta napkin and a patterned gold napkin. Iron napkins with generous amounts of spray starch before folding to help them hold their shape when arranged upright. This fold needs to be placed in a glass, so have one wineglass per napkin fold ready before you begin folding.

1 Lay the solid-color napkin out as a diamond, with the finished side facing down and the seamed edges facing up. Place the patterned napkin on top, with the finished side facing down and the seamed edges facing up, arranging it slightly lower than the solid-color napkin so that a bit of the solid-color napkin shows at the top of the diamond.

2 Fold the lower point of the patterned diamond up to the upper point of the patterned diamond, forming a patterned triangle atop a solid-color diamond.

3 Fold the lower point of the solid-color diamond up to just below the upper point of the patterned triangle, forming a triangle with three top points showing.

4 Holding the middle of the lower edge with your left hand, use your right hand to fold the right point up to the upper point.

5 Fold the left point up to the upper point, forming a diamond.

6 Fold the left edge of the right triangle down to the lower right edge, aligning the edges and leaving a tip extending to the right of the diamond.

7 Fold the right edge of the left triangle down to the lower left edge, aligning the edges and leaving a tip extending to the left of the diamond.

8 Flip the napkin fold over, keeping the same point down.

9 Fold the right half over to the left half, forming an arrow.

10 Working with the left side of the arrow, fold the top two layers over to the right side, leaving only solid napkin showing and maintaining the arrow shape.

11 Flip the napkin fold over, arranging it with the arrow pointing down.

12 Fold the right side of the arrow over the left side.

13 Tuck the lower tip up inside the napkin fold, using about one-third the length of the napkin.

14 Drop the bottom of the fold into a wineglass.

15 Gently separate and arrange the napkin fold's three points.

#100 Weave

Use this intricate fold anytime you want to show off your advanced napkin folding skills. A solid-color fabric will highlight the many interlocking layers best. Starch and press the napkins before you begin folding, and lightly press the finished fold for crisp results.

1 Lay the napkin out as a square, with the finished side facing down and the seamed edges facing up. Fold the lower edge up about 1 inch (2.5 cm), forming a band.

2 Holding the edges of the band and lifting it, form another band of the same height above the first one.

3 Holding the edges of both bands and lifting, reposition the bands higher on the napkin, forming another band of equal height below them.

4 Holding the edges of the three bands and lifting, reposition the bands higher on the napkin, forming another band of equal height above them.

5 Holding the edges of the four bands, lift the napkin and let the upper edge fall down underneath, so that it hangs down below the bands.

6 Tuck the loose edge under, leaving just enough showing at the lower edge to form the fifth band.

7 Smooth the bands.

8 Flip the napkin over, keeping the same edges at top and bottom.

9 Holding the middle 2 inches (5 cm) of the lower edge in place with your left hand, use your right hand to fold the right edge toward the upper left.

10 Fold the left edge toward the upper right, partially overlapping the right side.

11 Lifting all layers on the left side, top the innermost layer on the right side with the innermost layer of the left side.

12 Continue interweaving layers with the remaining three inside flaps.

13 Smooth the folds.

14 Flip the napkin over, keeping the same flat edge down. Fold the lower right edge over about 1 inch (2.5 cm), forming a band.

15 Fold the lower left edge over about 1 inch (2.5 cm), forming a band. Flip the napkin over again and arrange it with the narrow end at the top.

Index

Library and Archives Canada Cataloguing in Publication

Vivaldo, Denise
    Top 100 step-by-step napkin folds : more than 1,000 photographs / Denise Vivaldo.

Includes index.

ISBN 978-0-7788-0423-9

    1. Napkin folding. 2. Table setting and decoration. I. Title. II. Title: Top one hundred step-by-step napkin folds.

TX879.V585 2012   642'.79   C2012-902803-7

Entertaining Diary

Date	Menu	Guests
Table Setting Theme		
Napkin Fold(s) Used		
Notes		

Date	Menu	Guests
Table Setting Theme		
Napkin Fold(s) Used		
Notes		

Date	Menu	Guests
Table Setting Theme		
Napkin Fold(s) Used		
Notes		

Entertaining Diary

Date	Menu	Guests
Table Setting Theme		
Napkin Fold(s) Used		
Notes		

Date	Menu	Guests
Table Setting Theme		
Napkin Fold(s) Used		
Notes		

Date	Menu	Guests
Table Setting Theme		
Napkin Fold(s) Used		
Notes		